PERSEUS

PERSEUS

A Study in Greek Art and Legend

BY

JOCELYN M. WOODWARD

CAMBRIDGE

AT THE UNIVERSITY PRESS

1937

CAMBRIDGE UNIVERSITY PRESS
Cambridge, New York, Melbourne, Madrid, Cape Town,
Singapore, São Paulo, Delhi, Mexico City

Cambridge University Press
The Edinburgh Building, Cambridge CB2 8RU, UK

Published in the United States of America by Cambridge University Press, New York

www.cambridge.org
Information on this title: www.cambridge.org/9781107631243

First published 1937
First paperback edition 2013

A catalogue record for this publication is available from the British Library

ISBN 978-1-107-63124-3 Paperback

CONTENTS

ILLUSTRATIONS

TEXT-FIGURES

PLATES

vii

PREFACE

IT is my privilege to thank a number of people without whose help I could not have got together the material for this book. I am especially indebted to Miss Miriam Banks of the Rhode Island School of Design and to Professor Diepolder of Munich who were good enough to send me photographs specially taken for my purpose; to Mr F. N. Pryce of the British Museum, Professor Neugebauer of the Berlin Museum, Professor Merlin of the Louvre, Professor Cultrera of the Syracuse Museum and to the authorities of the Ashmolean, the Bibliothèque Nationale and the Bologna Museum who helped me to secure and allowed me to reproduce photographs of objects in the collections under their charge.

I have also to thank Professor Demangel, Professor Rumpf, the Council of the Hellenic Society, the German Archaeological Institute and l'Association pour l'encouragement des Études Grecques to whose kindness I owe a number of the illustrations.

The following generously allowed me to quote extracts or reproduce photographs from their publications: Messrs Macmillan and Co., the Editors of the Loeb Classical Library, the University of Michigan Press, Librairie Honoré Champion, Librairie Hachette, Éditions Cahiers d'Art, Presses Universitaires de France, Verlag Heinrich Keller and Verlag F. Bruckmann. In the list of references at the end of the book I hope I have acknowledged my indebtedness to the many publications I have consulted.

Miss Emilie Haspels and Miss Gladys Parkin read the manuscript and contributed much valuable criticism and advice, while my husband has had his full share in the discussion and solving of difficulties. Finally I must express my gratitude to the staff of the Cambridge University Press for their courtesy and expert help in matters of arrangement and reproduction.

June 1937   J. M. W.

INTRODUCTION

I HAVE put together the material in this book in the hopes that
it may partly fill a gap, or, at any rate, shew how big that gap
is. Kingsley's *Heroes* offers to all children their glorious first
sight of the Greek myths—but what is there to follow? With the
more advanced teaching of Latin and Greek in schools, language
and history are made the main study, while mythology and religion,
with their artistic expression, are usually left to a few lifeless words
in the notes or a hurried look at the Flaxmanised drawings of a
small classical dictionary. This is bound to be the case when the
material for the study is so difficult to get at, for it is, most of it,
published in periodicals or in expensive books of reference, many
of them foreign.

This really gives a disproportionate view of Greek life and a
Greek would have been puzzled and indignant to know that, while
we studied his verbs with such reverence, his cherished legends
were either ignored or remembered only as lovely fairy-tales for
children.

At a later period, certainly, the educated Greek would feel a
little apologetic about the more imaginative tales, but to the
Greeks who fought back the Persian invasion, these stories were
too wrapped up in the sudden, flowerlike glory of their country
to seem in any way impossible or fantastic. These heroes whose
deeds were pictured in marble on every temple, whose statues
stood everywhere, in the holy precincts, in the streets and por-
ticoes, were no mere shadows of a poet's fancy.

The Olympian gods indeed had their temples and ceremonies,
but there was a great deal more than this. All over the country

were the shrines and tombs of the heroes and heroines of early days, who seem to have filled a part very much like that filled by the saints of the Christian church.

Each shrine would have its festival at a certain season of the year, with special ritual of purification, song or sacrifice, and even though, to most of the worshippers, it probably meant largely dancing and cakes and wine, there was none the less a genuine belief in the reason for it all.

These stories of the past played a very real part in the life of a Greek. In almost every chapter of his famous *Description of Greece* Pausanias makes mention of the cult or shrine of some hero. The great Games at Olympia were held in honour of the dead hero, Pelops; Theseus's tomb in Athens was a refuge for slaves and the oppressed and a solemn ritual commemorated each year the day of his return from Crete; Perseus was honoured near Mycenae and in Seriphos; Helen had her festival in Laconia; at Troezen it was the custom that every maiden, before marriage, should cut off a lock of her hair and dedicate it in the temple of Hippolytos. A grim ritual is recorded from Locri, whose citizens had to send each year, in expiation of Ajax's crime against Cassandra long ago, two maidens, chosen by lot, to Athena's temple in Ilion, where, if they were not slain by the inhabitants of the place, they were held captive for life. It was not just all make-believe; men do not do such things for the sake of what they think is only a picturesque nursery tale.

In this book I have taken only the legend of Perseus and have put together, from ancient writers, some of the passages that deal with it. With these are figured a few from the great number of the artistic representations of the story, arranged, not in the order of the events in the story, but according to their place in the history of art, and though they do not represent every phase or style, they form a more or less connected series and may prove good landmarks to anyone who is making a first study of classical art. They must not be regarded merely as illustrations to the literary story. There was a great common source of national tradition which artist and poet alike could draw upon and which each was free to use in his own way. The vase-painter's presentation of a myth is as good authority as the written word and often brings out an aspect that has been lost in the poet's different treatment of the subject.

There is no need to draw anyone's attention to the vivid narrative power of most of these art monuments or to the skill with which the scenes are adapted to the different media of stone or clay. But there is another thing that only comes out when the pictures are grouped together in this way: they reflect so truthfully the mental attitude of the artist towards the legend, and through him the mental attitude of the ordinary, everyday citizen who liked and bought his work. (For we must remember that the vase-paintings from which this selection is mainly drawn were made to meet the popular demand and not only for a few discerning patrons. Their makers won no fame as artists—no classical writer has thought it worth while to record the name of any vase-painter.) First we have the crude, grim earnestness of the early archaic work; then later the delight in the sheer beauty of the figures, their movements and grouping, leading to the dignity and ethical grandeur of the Periclean age; and finally all the polished romance and appeal to sentiment of the work of the Hellenistic age. Such changes of taste cannot come about without some cause; there are corresponding changes in political conditions and in social life to account for them, and when we are studying the history of a nation for whom art and the artistic expression of their feelings were among the citizen's ordinary, daily occupations, we should not forget the importance of these vase-paintings and sculptures as vital contemporary documents.

THE STORY OF PERSEUS IN
GREEK LITERATURE

THE STORY OF PERSEUS IN
GREEK LITERATURE

THERE are many references to the story of Perseus in Greek literature. How much Homer knew of it, we cannot say; he only makes bare mention of the names of Perseus, Danae and the Gorgon. But from the evidence of the poems of Hesiod and Simonides, it is clear that the main details of the Gorgon and Danae stories were established at an early date, and probably there once existed an epic poem that gave form to the myth, though no trace of such a poem has survived.

The story of Andromeda does not appear in literature till later, but the vase shewn in Fig. 9 is evidence that her story was already popular in the sixth century B.C. and it seems that at an early time she took her place among the stars (cf. p. 22).

It is interesting to find the story of the Gorgon's head so rounded off and complete at such an early stage of its history. It is not just the long string of unconnected adventures that Greek mythology so often has to offer; it has form and pattern—a pattern that is familiar to us in many fairy-tales, where the hero, before he comes to his final task, must first fulfil, as he does here, some minor test— to scale a mountain or to find the magic flower—and the old woman or the dwarf who shews him the way and the magic gifts that are to help him are old friends.

Writers of a later, critical age try to rationalise the story, but their laboured explanations are far more fantastic than any myth. Pausanias records some curious details which may partly have grown out of attempts to give importance to obscure local legends by linking them up with the more famous Perseus story.

It is a mistake to read a deep moral interpretation into the tale. It is not the Greek way. To the Greeks the Perseus legend was no more than a fine story about one of their heroes who once lived[1] and who was especially active in clearing the world of strange and dangerous monsters. There does not seem to have been any laborious interpretation of the story as the victory of Good over Evil, and when the Greek artist uses it as material for his art there is no kind of moral symbolism to obscure the direct artistic appeal of his work. The following are some of the most interesting references in literature:

PHERECYDES

The stories of Acrisios, Danae and the quest of the Gorgon's head, though not that of Andromeda, are told most fully in the account written by Pherecydes. Tradition about him is confused. There seems to have been more than one writer of that name. The writer of these passages most probably lived in Athens in the first half of the fifth century B.C. He wrote a long work in prose about Greek mythology which is lost, but many passages from it are quoted by ancient writers and give us some idea of its character.

In writing a commentary on Apollonius Rhodius, *Argonautica*, an ancient scholar quotes the following passages from Pherecydes:

In a note on *Argonautica*, IV. 1091 (*Frag. Hist. Graec.* I. 75, fr. 26).

Pherecydes, in his second book, says that Acrisios married Eurydice, daughter of Lacedaimon, and they had a daughter, Danae. Acrisios consulted the oracle as to whether he would have a son, and the Pythian God replied that he would never have a son himself but that his daughter

[1] When Xerxes was preparing to invade Greece he appealed to the men of Argos not to join with the rest of the Greeks against him, on the strength of his kinship with them through their common ancestor, Perseus, from whose son, Perses, the Persian kings were said to be descended. Cf. Herodotus, VII. 150 and p. 7, note 2.

4

would have one at whose hand he was destined to die. So he went home to Argos and built a bronze chamber underground in the court-yard of his house, and there he put Danae and her nurse and kept her there so that she might not bear a son. But Zeus fell in love with the maiden and descended from the roof in a shower of gold. And she gave birth to a son, Perseus, and, with the help of her nurse, reared him in secret. When Perseus was three or four years old Acrisios heard his voice as he was playing and he sent servants to fetch Danae and her nurse; he killed the nurse and dragged Danae with her child to the altar of Zeus, Guardian of the Threshold, and when he was alone with her he asked her who was the father of her son. When she answered "Zeus", he would not believe her and put her in a chest with her child and shut it down and cast it on the sea. It floated away and came to the island of Seriphos. Dictys, son of Peristhenes, rescued them, catching the chest with his fishing-net. Then Danae begged him to open the chest and he opened it, and, learning who they were, he took them to his home and kept them as they were of his own kin.[1]

In a note on *Argonautica*, IV. 1515 (*Frag. Hist. Graec.* I. 75, fr. 26).

Perseus lived with his mother in the house of Dictys and came to manhood, then one day Polydectes, Dictys's brother, who was king of Seriphos, saw Danae and fell in love with her, yet did not know how he should lay hands on her. He prepared a feast[2] and invited to it Perseus and many others. Perseus asked what gift he should bring to the feast, and when Polydectes replied "A horse", Perseus retorted "The Gorgon's head".

After the feast, on the following day, the rest of the guests each brought a horse and Perseus did the same. But Polydectes would not receive his horse but demanded the Gorgon's head as he had promised. If he did not bring it, he declared, he would take his mother captive. Perseus, sad at heart and lamenting his unhappy fate, went off to the

[1] Dictys and Danae were both descended from Danaus, an early king of Argos.
[2] "Under the pretext of collecting contributions towards a wedding-gift for Hippodameia, daughter of Oenomaos." Apollodorus, II. iv. 2.

far end of the island. There Hermes appeared to him, questioned him and learned the reason of his sorrow. He told him to be of good cheer and led him, under Athena's directions, to the Graiae, daughters of Phorcys, Pemphredo, Enyo and Dino. He stole from them their eye and tooth as they were handing them from one to another, and when they found out what had happened, they cried aloud and begged him to give them back the eye and the tooth. For they only had the one between them and they used it in turn. And Perseus said he had them and would give them back on condition that they would shew him the way to the Nymphs who keep the cap of Hades, the winged sandals and the bag (*kibisis*). So they told him and he gave them back the eye and the tooth. Then, with Hermes, he went to the Nymphs and made his request, and he received the things and fastened the winged sandals to his feet, slung the bag about his shoulders and set the cap of Hades on his head.[1] Then he flew to Ocean, to the Gorgons, and Hermes and Athena went with him. He found the Gorgons sleeping. And the Gods warned him that he must turn away as he cut off the Gorgon's head and, in a mirror, they shewed him Medusa, the only one of the Gorgons who was mortal. He drew near and cut off her head with the *harpe*, put it in his bag and fled.[2] When the Gorgons found what had happened they pursued him but they could not see him as he was wearing the cap of Hades.

Perseus reached Seriphos and, going to Polydectes, bade him summon the people together that he might shew them the Gorgon's head, well knowing that if they looked on it they would be turned to stone. Polydectes summoned the people together and bade him shew them the head. Then Perseus turned away, drew the head out of the bag and held it up. As they gazed on it they were turned to stone.

Athena took the head from Perseus and set it in her aegis. He

---

[1] "Having received also from Hermes an adamantine sickle (*harpe*)." Apoll. ii. iv. 2.

[2] "And while Athena guided his hand and he looked with averted gaze on a brazen shield in which he beheld the image of the Gorgon, he beheaded her. When her head was cut off, there sprang from the Gorgon the winged horse Pegasos and Chrysaor, the father of Geryon." Apoll. ii. iv. 2.

6

gave the bag back to Hermes, and the sandals and the cap to the Nymphs.[1]

Pherecydes relates this in his second book.

In a note on *Argonautica*, IV. 1090 (*Frag. Hist. Graec.* I. 76, fr. 26).

After this Pherecydes goes on to tell of the death of Acrisios. After Polydectes and his followers were turned to stone by the Gorgon's head in Seriphos, Perseus left Dictys in Seriphos to reign over the people who were left alive and he himself took ship and sailed to Argos with the Cyclopes, with Danae and with Andromeda. And when he got there, he did not find Acrisios in Argos for, in fear of him, he had fled to the Pelasgians in Larissa. Not finding his grandfather in Argos, Perseus left Danae with her mother, Eurydice, and Andromeda and the Cyclopes also. He himself went off to Larissa. When he got there he recognised Acrisios and persuaded him to come back to Argos with him. Just as they were setting out, it happened that they were holding an athletic contest among the young men of Larissa. Perseus stripped for the contest, took hold of the discus and threw it, and the discus flew against the foot of Acrisios and crushed it. And Acrisios died of the wound there in Larissa. Perseus and the men of Larissa buried him before the city, and the people built him a shrine. And Perseus returned to Argos.[2]

[1] "But it is alleged by some that Medusa was beheaded for Athena's sake; and they say that the Gorgon was fain to match herself with the goddess even in beauty." Apoll. II. iv. 3.

[2] "And being ashamed to return to Argos to claim the inheritance of him who had died by his hand, he went to Megapenthes, son of Proetus, at Tiryns and effected an exchange with him, surrendering Argos into his hands. So Megapenthes reigned over the Argives, and Perseus reigned over Tiryns, after fortifying also Midea and Mycenae. And he had sons by Andromeda: before he came to Greece he had Perses, whom he left behind with Cepheus (and from him it is said that the kings of Persia are descended); and in Mycenae he had Alcaeus and Sthenelus and Heleus and Mestor and Electryon, and a daughter Gorgophone, whom Perieres married." Apoll. II. iv. 4.

APOLLODORUS

We find further details and the full story of the rescue of Andromeda in the *Library* of Apollodorus. Beyond his writings there is nothing known about this Apollodorus, though there is reason to believe that he lived in either the first or the second century A.D. In the *Library* he has evidently used the works of several earlier writers and made a valuable summary of most of the legends of the Greeks. I do not give his version of the slaying of Medusa, for it agrees very closely with the one of Pherecydes. I have quoted, in notes on Pherecydes's version, a few of the passages where Apollodorus differs from it; in some of these, as in the story of Medusa's rivalry with Athena, one can clearly see the more sophisticated taste of a later generation.

It is probable that the following account of Andromeda's rescue is also based on the work of Pherecydes, on some passage which has not been preserved.

APOLLODORUS, II. iv. 3.[1]

Being come to Ethiopia, of which Cepheus was king, he found the king's daughter Andromeda set out to be the prey of a sea monster. For Cassiepea, the wife of Cepheus, vied with the Nereids in beauty and boasted to be better than them all; hence the Nereids were angry, and Poseidon, sharing their wrath, sent a flood and a monster to invade the land. But Ammon having predicted deliverance from the calamity if Cassiepea's daughter Andromeda were exposed as a prey to the monster, Cepheus was compelled by the Ethiopians to do it, and he bound his daughter to a rock. When Perseus beheld her, he loved her and promised Cepheus that he would kill the monster, if he would give him the rescued

[1] From the translation by Sir J. G. Frazer (Loeb Classical Library).

8

damsel to wife. These terms having been sworn to, Perseus with-
stood and slew the monster and released Andromeda. However,
Phineus, who was a brother of Cepheus, and to whom Andromeda
had been first betrothed, plotted against him; but Perseus discovered the plot, and by shewing the Gorgon turned him and his
fellow-conspirators at once into stone.

HESIOD

The most picturesque account of the slaying of the Gorgon appears
in Hesiod's *Shield of Heracles*, dating perhaps as early as the eighth
century B.C., a Boeotian poem, a late echo of the great age of epic
poetry. It tells of the birth of Heracles and how he slew Cycnus,
son of Ares, in the grove of Apollo at Pagasae in Thessaly.

The poem is chiefly made up of the description of his shield
and the figures on it in imitation of the famous Shield of Achilles
(*Iliad*, XVIII. 478 ff.). It has some lovely lines of vivid detail and
flashes of things seen with a poet's eye, but it is ineptly piled
together and the poet is clearly out of his depth in this heroic
setting. The story of Perseus is well told with all the rich detail
of "What was it like?" and "What was it made of?" that is the
essence of a good story to a nation in its childhood.

HESIOD, *Shield of Heracles*, 216 ff.[1]

There too was the son of rich-haired Danae, the horseman Perseus:
his feet did not touch the shield and yet were not far from it—
very marvellous to remark, since he was not supported anywhere;
for so did the famous Lame One[2] fashion him of gold with his
hands. On his feet he had winged sandals, and his black-sheathed
sword was slung across his shoulders by a cross-belt of bronze.

---

[1] From the translation by H. G. Evelyn-White (Loeb Classical Library).
[2] Hephaestos.

He was flying swift as thought. The head of a dreadful monster, the Gorgon, covered the broad of his back, and a bag of silver— a marvel to see—contained it: and from the bag bright tassels of gold hung down. Upon the head of the hero lay the dread cap of Hades which had the awful gloom of night. Perseus himself, the son of Danae, was at full stretch, like one who hurries and shudders with horror. And after him rushed the Gorgons, unapproachable and unspeakable, longing to seize him: as they trod upon the pale adamant, the shield rang sharp and clear with a loud clanging. Two serpents hung down at their girdles with heads curved forward: their tongues were flickering, and their teeth gnashing with fury, and their eyes glaring fiercely. And upon the awful heads of the Gorgons great Fear was quaking.

HESIOD, *Theogony*, 270 ff.

And again, Ceto bare to Phorcys the fair-cheeked Graiae, sisters grey from their birth: and both deathless gods and men who walk on earth call them Graiae, Pemphredo well-clad, and saffron-robed Enyo, and the Gorgons who dwell beyond glorious Ocean in the frontier land towards Night where are the clear-voiced Hesperides, Sthenno, and Euryale, and Medusa[1] who suffered a woeful fate: she was mortal, but the two were undying and grew not old. With her lay the Dark-haired One[2] in a soft meadow amid spring flowers. And when Perseus cut off her head, there sprang forth great Chrysaor and the horse Pegasos, who is so called because he was born near the springs (*pegae*) of Ocean; and that other, because he held a golden blade (*aor*) in his hands.

---

[1] *Sthenno*, The Mighty One; *Euryale*, The Far-leaping; *Medusa*, The Vanquisher.
[2] Poseidon.

SIMONIDES

The lyric age, sensitive and personal, that succeeds the epic in Greece has left us one lovely fragment inspired by the Perseus legend—Simonides's famous lament of Danae. Simonides (556–467 B.C.) of Keos wrote lyrics of many forms—we know him best from the lines written in honour of the Lacedaemonians who fell at Thermopylae. In this fragment, probably part of a long poem, the metre is intricate and cannot be approached in English verse, but the prose version gives some idea of its tenderness and emotional appeal, a contrast to the sturdy narrative of the preceding epic piece. It is an irony that this fragment is only preserved to us because a literary critic of the first century B.C. quotes it to prove how near lyric composition can be to prose, saying that if the lines of this poem were not written in verse form it would be difficult to grasp the rhythm of it.

SIMONIDES, Fr. 27 (Bergk 37).[1]

When the wind came blowing upon the carven chest and the swaying sea bent her towards fear and tears that would not be stayed from her cheeks, she threw a loving arm round Perseus, saying, "O babe, what woe is thine! and yet thou weepest not, but slumberest in thy suckling's way as thou liest night-bound in the black darkness of a dismal brass-ribbed bark, and reckest not of the salt of the passing wave so thick on thy hair, nay, nor the cry of the wind, lying in thy purple swathings with thy pretty face against me. For if the dire were dire to thee, thou'dst lend thy little ear to what I say. So sleep thou on, my baby, as I pray the sea may sleep and our great, great woe may sleep; and come some

[1] From the translation by J. M. Edmonds (Loeb Classical Library).

change to us, Father Zeus, of thee. And whatsoever of my prayer be overbold and wrong, do thou forgive it me."

PINDAR

Pindar, living about the time of the Persian wars, a poet of Boeotia, as Hesiod was, writes lyrics in a grander, more heroic strain—hymns to the gods and choral odes in honour of the victors in the public games. In his odes he makes much use of myths. As he says, "The pride of these songs of praise speedeth from tale to tale as bee from flower to flower", and he piles up his imagery so recklessly with the ideas hurrying one upon another, that to us, without the music and gesture that must originally have accompanied the poem, the connection of thought is often hard to follow. This ode was written to be sung in honour of a boy from Thessaly who had won the boys' race in the festival at Delphi in 498 B.C., and Pindar gives it colour by introducing a stage in Perseus's journey that we do not find related elsewhere—his visit to the Hyperboreans, the mysterious people who dwell "beyond the North Wind".

PINDAR, *Pythian*, X. 29.[1]

Yet neither on shipboard nor by land-faring couldst thou find the
    wondrous road to the gathering of the Hyperborean folk:
Into whose homes Perseus, the leader of the people, entered and
    joined their feasts,
Having found them offering goodly hekatombs of asses to the God:
In whose revels and holy speech Apollo taketh great delight.
The Muse is no stranger there in their rule of life,
And everywhere the singing-bands of maidens, the voices of the
    lyres, the trills of flutes throb in their ears;

---

[1] From *The Works of Pindar*, L. R. Farnell (Macmillan & Co.).

12

And having bound their locks in golden laurel they hold festival
in gladness of soul.
Neither age nor wasting sickness is the portion of that holy race;
But they live far aloof from toil and battle,
Freed from the o'erstrict judgment-court of Nemesis.
Of old came the son of Danae, kindled with boldness of spirit,
And Athena led him on to the fellowship of these happy men.
He slew the Gorgon, and farèd back, bearing to the islanders the
head with its speckled snake-locks, the Terror that froze to
stone.

LUCIAN

The following passage takes us back to a time when the satiric
dialogue was a new and exciting discovery in literary form. Lucian
(second century A.D.), as he proudly says, was the first to "wed
Comedy with Dialogue"; for before his time the dialogue form
had been used only in philosophical writings such as the Dialogues
of Plato. Lucian now uses the prose conversation form for lighter,
more amusing subjects, usually with a strong vein of satire. This
is rather a ponderous example of his wit; he can sometimes drive
his points home in a much more drastic and outspoken way.

LUCIAN, *Dialogues of the Sea-Gods*, XIV.[1]

TRITON. IPHIANASSA. DORIS. NEREIDS.

Tri. Well, ladies: so the monster you sent against the daughter
of Cepheus has got killed himself, and never done Andromeda any
harm at all!

Nereid. Who did it? I suppose Cepheus was just using his
daughter as a bait, and had a whole army waiting in ambush to
kill him?

[1] From the translation by H. W. Fowler and F. G. Fowler (Oxford, Clarendon
Press).

13

Tri. No, no,—Iphianassa, you remember Perseus, Danae's boy? —they were both thrown into the sea by the boy's grandfather, in that chest, you know, and you took pity on them.

Iph. I know; why, I suppose he is a fine handsome young fellow by now?

Tri. It was he who killed your monster.

Iph. But why? This was not the way to shew his gratitude.

Tri. I'll tell you all about it. The king had sent him on this expedition against the Gorgons, and when he got to Libya—

Iph. How did he get there? all by himself? he must have had someone to help him?—it is a dangerous journey otherwise.

Tri. He flew,—Athene gave him wings.—Well, so when he got to where the Gorgons were living, he caught them napping, I suppose, cut off Medusa's head, and flew away.

Iph. How could he see them? The Gorgons are a forbidden sight. Whoever looks at them will never look at anyone else again.

Tri. Athene held up her shield—I heard him telling Andromeda and Cepheus about it afterwards—Athene showed him the reflection of the Gorgon in her shield, which is as bright as any mirror; so he took hold of her hair in his left hand, grasped his scimitar with the right, still looking at the reflection, cut off her head, and was off before her sisters woke up. Lowering his flight as he reached the Ethiopian coast yonder, he caught sight of Andromeda, fettered to a jutting rock, her hair hanging loose about her shoulders; ye Gods, what loveliness was there exposed to view! And first pity of her hard fate prompted him to ask the cause of her doom: but Fate had decreed the maiden's deliverance, and presently Love stole upon him, and he resolved to save her. The hideous monster now drew near, and would have swallowed her: but the youth, hovering above, smote him with the drawn scimitar in his right hand, and with his left uncovered the petri-

14

fying Gorgon's head: in one moment the monster was lifeless; all of him that had met that gaze was turned to stone. Then Perseus released the maiden from her fetters, and supported her, as with timid steps she descended from the slippery rock.—And now he is to marry her in Cepheus's palace, and take her home to Argos; so that where she looked for death, she has found an uncommonly good match.

Iph. I am not sorry to hear it. It is no fault of hers, if her mother has the vanity to set up for our rival.

Dor. Still, she *is* Andromeda's mother; and we should have had our revenge on her through the daughter.

Iph. My dear, let bygones be bygones. What matter if a barbarian queen's tongue runs away with her? She is sufficiently punished by the fright. So let us take this marriage in good part.

PAUSANIAS

Sometime in the second half of the second century A.D., Pausanias made a tour of Greece, and the ten books of his famous *Description of Greece* are the results of his notes and researches. It is a treasure-house of information of all kinds. He must have been a most painstaking tourist—never too tired to visit each place of interest and noting down all he heard about the local antiquities, legends and religious ceremonies. He consults numerous ancient authorities and sifts the evidence; sometimes he quotes his information as he hears it from the local guide, sometimes, as in II. xxi. 5, he makes stern efforts to rationalise the fantastic side of the myth. In some of the passages quoted here one can almost hear the rattle of the keys and the chink of the extra coin in the guide's hand as he unlocks a side door and produces special information for this persistent sightseer.

PAUSANIAS, I. xxi. 3.[1]

On what is called the south wall of the Acropolis (at Athens), which faces towards the theatre, there is a gilded head of the Gorgon Medusa, and round about the head is wrought an aegis.

PAUSANIAS, I. xxii. 4–6.

There is but one entrance to the Acropolis: it admits of no other, being everywhere precipitous and fortified with a strong wall. The portal (Propylaea) has a roof of white marble, and for the beauty and size of the blocks it has never yet been matched....On the left of the portal is a chamber containing pictures....Amongst other paintings there is a picture of Alcibiades containing emblems of the victory won by his team at Nemea. Perseus is also depicted on his way back to Seriphos, carrying the head of Medusa to Polydectes. But I do not care to tell the story of Medusa in treating of Attica.

PAUSANIAS, I. xxiii. 7.

Among other things that I saw on the Acropolis at Athens were the bronze boy holding the sprinkler, and Perseus after he has done the deed on Medusa. The boy is a work of Lycius, son of Myron: the Perseus is a work of Myron.

PAUSANIAS, II. xvi. 3.

When Perseus returned to Argos, ashamed at the notoriety of the homicide, he persuaded Megapenthes, son of Proetus, to change kingdoms with him. So when he had received the kingdom of Proetus he founded Mycenae, because there the cap (*mykes*) of his scabbard had fallen off, and he regarded this as a sign to found a city. I have also heard that being thirsty he chanced to take up a

[1] From the translation by Sir J. G. Frazer, *Pausanias's Description of Greece* (Macmillan & Co.).

mushroom (*mykes*) and that water flowing from it he drank, and being pleased gave the place the name of Mycenae.

PAUSANIAS, II. xviii. 1.

On the way from Mycenae to Argos is a shrine[1] of the hero Perseus beside the road on the left. He is honoured here by the people of the neighbourhood; but he is most honoured in Seriphos.

PAUSANIAS, II. xx. 7.

(At Argos) beside the sanctuary of Cephisus is a head of Medusa made of stone: they say that it too is a work of the Cyclopes.

PAUSANIAS, II. xxi. 5, 6.

Not far from the building in the market-place of Argos is a mound of earth: they say that in it lies the head of the Gorgon Medusa. If we leave out the mythical element, the story told of her is this: she was a daughter of Phorcus, and when her father died she reigned over the people who dwell round about the Lake Tritonis. She used to go out hunting, and she led the Libyans to battle. But being encamped with her army over against the host of Perseus, who was accompanied by picked troops from Peloponnese, she was assassinated by night, and Perseus, admiring her beauty even in death, cut off her head and brought it to show to the Greeks. But a Carthaginian named Procles, the son of Eucrates, thought that the following account was more plausible. The desert of Libya

---

[1] A stone has actually been found at Mycenae bearing an inscription which refers to "the priests of Perseus" (*Ephemeris Archaiologike*, 1892, p. 67), and a series of coins of Argos, of Roman Imperial date (see text-figure above), bear a figure of Perseus with Gorgon's head and *harpe* which may have some connection with a statue at this shrine. (Text-figure = *Journal of Hellenic Studies*, VI. 1885, p. 84, Pl. I, xviii.)

contains wild beasts, such as a man would not believe in if he were told of them; and amongst these monsters are wild men and wild women. Procles said that he had seen one of these men who had been brought to Rome. He conjectured, therefore, that one of these women had wandered to the Lake Tritonis, and there harried the people of the neighbourhood till Perseus slew her; and because the people who dwell round about the Lake Tritonis are sacred to Athena, it was supposed that the goddess had aided him in his exploit.

PAUSANIAS, II. xxiii. 7.

There are other things worth seeing at Argos; for instance, an underground structure,[1] over which was the brazen chamber which Acrisios made to imprison his daughter in. But when Perilaus made himself tyrant he pulled it down.

PAUSANIAS, IV. XXXV. 9.

Water may assume every hue and smell. The bluest water I ever saw was the water at Thermopylae, not all of it, only the water that descends into the swimming-bath which the natives call the Women's Pots. Red water, red as blood, may be seen in the land of the Hebrews, near the city of Joppa. The water is hard by the sea, and the local legend runs that when Perseus had slain the sea-beast, to which the daughter of Cepheus was exposed, he washed off the blood at this spring.

PAUSANIAS, VIII. xlvii. 5.

There is another sanctuary of Athena at Tegea, that of Athena Poliatis ("Guardian of the City"): once each year a priest enters it. They name it the Sanctuary of the Bulwark, saying that to Cepheus, son of Aleus, a boon was granted by Athena, that Tegea should

---

[1] Perhaps the remains of a beehive tomb like those at Mycenae.

never be taken; and they say that the goddess cut off some of the hair of Medusa and gave him it as a means of guarding the city.

PAUSANIAS, IX. xxxiv. 2.

(Of the sanctuary of Itonian Athena at Boeotian Koroneia) the following story is told: Iodama, priestess of the goddess, entered the precinct by night, and Athena appeared to her; but on the goddess's tunic was the head of the Gorgon Medusa, and when Iodama saw it she was turned to stone. Therefore a woman places fire every day on the altar of Iodama, and as she does so she says thrice in the Boeotian dialect that Iodama is alive and asks for fire.

ATHENAEUS

Athenaeus (end of the second century A.D.), living in an age of compilers and dictionary-makers, gives us an extraordinary jumble of information in his *Deipnosophistae* ("Learned Men at Dinner"). It consists of fifteen books, written in the form of a conversation at dinner, and not only deals with cooking and wine and all the accessories of a banquet but introduces discussions and anecdotes on every subject conceivable. He quotes many passages from early authors, and here he gives a description of the Gorgon, which seems to be rather an odd thing to come from an "Inquiry into Birds".

ATHENAEUS, *Deipnosophistae*, v. 221.[1]

"And speaking of Gorgons, Alexander of Myndus records that certain animals really exist capable of turning men into stone. In the second book of his *Inquiry into Birds* he says: 'The gorgon is the creature which the Numidians of Libya, where it occurs, call "down-looker". As the majority aver, drawing their comparison from its skin, it is like a wild sheep; but some say that it is like a calf. They say, too, that it has a breath so strong that it destroys

[1] From the translation by C. B. Gulick (Loeb Classical Library).

anyone who meets the animal. And it carries a mane hanging from its forehead over the eyes; whenever it shakes this aside, as it does with difficulty because of its weight, and catches sight of anything, it kills whatever is seen by it; not by its breath, but by the influence which emanates from the peculiar nature of its eyes; and it turns the object into a corpse. It came to be known in this wise. Some soldiers in the expedition of Marius against Jugurtha saw the gorgon, and supposing that it was a wild sheep, since its head was bent low and it moved slowly, they rushed forward to get it, thinking that they could kill it with what swords they had. But the creature, being startled, shook the mane which lay over its eyes and immediately turned to corpses the men who had rushed upon it. Again and again other persons did the same thing and became corpses; and since all who attacked it at close quarters always died, some made inquiry of the natives about the nature of the animal; whereupon some Numidian horsemen, at the command of Marius, lay in ambush for it at a distance and shot it; they then returned with the animal to the commander.' That this creature was, to be sure, of the character described is certified both by its skin and by the expedition under Marius. But that other report given by this investigator is not credible; he says that in Libya there are backward-grazing cattle, so called because they do not move forward when they graze, but do it retreating backwards; for, says he, their horns are a hindrance to grazing in the natural way, since they do not curve upwards like those of all other animals, but incline downwards and shade their eyes. This is really incredible, since no other inquirer confirms it."

These remarks of Ulpian[1] were confirmed and attested in so many words by Larensis,[1] who said that Marius had sent skins of these animals back to Rome, and that no one could guess to what

---

[1] Characters taking part in the conversation.

animal they belonged, so extraordinary was their appearance; he further said that these skins hang dedicated in the temple of Hercules.

STRABO

STRABO, *Geographica*, X. 5. 10.

And there is Seriphos, where, as the story goes, Dictys drew to land with his nets the chest in which were Perseus and his mother, Danae, who had been cast out to sea by Acrisios, the father of Danae. The story goes that Perseus grew up there and that when he brought the Gorgon's head he shewed it to the Seriphians and turned them all to stone. This he did to avenge his mother, for Polydectes, the king, with their help, purposed to marry her against her will.

The island is so rocky that the comic actors say that it was the Gorgon's head that made it so.

AELIAN

AELIAN, *De Natura Animalium*, III. 37.

In Seriphos you never hear the frogs croak at all and yet, if you take them to some other place, they croak loud and shrill. About their frogs, the people of Seriphos boast that Perseus came back from his victory over the Gorgon after journeying over many lands and, being tired as was only natural, he rested by the lake and lay down to sleep. But the frogs started croaking and annoyed the hero and interrupted his sleep. Then Perseus begged his father to silence them. Zeus hearkened to him and granted his son's prayer and condemned the frogs of the place to perpetual silence. But Theophrastus rejects the tradition and denies the boast of the people of Seriphos, for he says that the coldness of the water is the reason of the frogs' silence.

JOSEPHUS

JOSEPHUS, *History of the Jewish War*, III. ix. 3.[1]

Nature has not provided Joppa with a port. It terminates in a rugged shore, which runs for nearly its whole length in a straight line, but is slightly curved at its two extremities in crescent fashion; these horns consist of steep cliffs and reefs jutting far out into the deep; here are still shewn the impressions of Andromeda's chains, to attest the antiquity of that legend.

PSEUDO-ERATOSTHENES

PSEUDO-ERATOSTHENES, *Katasterismi* ("Figures in the Stars"), 15 ff.

Cepheus, as Euripides says, was king of the Ethiopians and father of Andromeda. It seems that he exposed his daughter to feed the monster and Perseus, son of Zeus, saved her, wherefore Cepheus too, by the will of Athena, was set among the stars....

Cassiepeia...is placed near by, sitting on a chair....

Andromeda was set by Athena among the stars as a memorial of the deeds of Perseus, with her arms outspread, as she was exposed to the monster....Euripides clearly speaks of it in his drama written about her....

Athena set Perseus among the stars, where he can be seen holding the Gorgon's head....

The Monster is what Poseidon sent against Cepheus because Cassiepeia vied with the Nereids in beauty. Perseus killed it and for this reason it was set among the stars as a memorial of his deed. Sophocles, the tragic poet, tells of this in the *Andromeda*.

[1] From the translation by H. St J. Thackeray (Loeb Classical Library).

JOHN OF ANTIOCH

The learning and research of the fourth century A.D. brought with it the sceptics. Various writers try to rationalise the story of Perseus, but their interpretations are most of them very dull and silly. John of Antioch, writing, it is supposed, about the beginning of the sixth century A.D., compiled a wonderful conglomerate history incorporating some of these versions and large parts of his work have survived. He begins with the story of Adam, puts the Greek gods into the family of Noah and shews us, among other things, King David refusing to send help to Priam of Troy.

His account rationalises all the Greek wonders in a most ruthless fashion: Heracles becomes a philosopher, vanquishing evil desire with the club of Philosophy: the Golden Fleece becomes a book, written on vellum, telling how to make gold by alchemy. The story of the Gorgon is treated in the same common-sense manner.

JOHN OF ANTIOCH (*Frag. Hist. Graec.* IV. 539, fr. 1, 8).
The Gorgon was a lovely courtesan who, by her beauty, filled all who looked on her with amazement so that they seemed to be turned to stone. And Pegasos was a swift horse that belonged to her. But Palaiphatos says that it was the name of Bellerophon's ship.

JOHN OF ANTIOCH (*Frag. Hist. Graec.* IV. 544, fr. 6, 18).
And Perseus quarrelled with the father of Andromeda who was old and blind. And, as he was used to do, he held up the Gorgon's head in defence. But as Cepheus was blind, it had no effect on him. Perseus, who could not understand why the old man escaped death at sight of the Gorgon, thought that the head which he held must have lost its power, turned it towards himself, looked on it and perished. And his son, Merros, ruled over the Persians after him and he it was who burnt that dreadful Gorgon's head.

THE STORY OF PERSEUS
IN GREEK ART

FIGURES 1 *a* and *b*. METOPES OF PAINTED CLAY from Thermon in Aetolia. Athens, National Museum. Corinthian, second half of the seventh century B.C. (ht. about 88 cm.)[1]

THOUGH Attic vase-painters were later to be supreme in Greece so that they monopolised the entire trade with their fine pottery, it was not until well into the sixth century that they began to take the lead. In the middle of the seventh century, when Athens was only just feeling her way to a real artistic sense, Corinth was already producing pottery of well-balanced design and exquisite workmanship. It was Corinth that first learnt to work in the black-figure style that was to become so famous later in the hands of Attic artists, and at this time Corinthian wares dominated the markets of the Greek world; they have been found in places as far afield as Marseilles, Carthage and South Russia.

In ancient writers we find many references to the fame of early Corinthian painting—that is free painting, for the decoration of walls and other large surfaces—and probably these larger works had much to do with the excellence of the smaller art of the vase-painter. But it is difficult to gauge the value of literary traditions about painting when so little of this kind of work has survived. The large plaques of painted clay from Thermon, two of which are figured here, are among the few precious examples we have.

In 1897, in a remote part of Aetolia, on the hills above the lake of Agrinion, Greek excavators unearthed the remains of a temple sacred to Apollo, of seventh-century date, built of clay bricks and wood and lavishly decorated with moulded and painted terracotta. A row of life-size heads in relief, alternating with lions' masks, decorated the gutter, and great painted slabs were set in the frieze to take the place of the sculptured metopes of stone-

---

[1] A list of references to the illustrations is given at the end of the book, pp. 94–96.

built temples (cf. Fig. 15 b). The painting is undoubtedly Corinthian work and it is striking evidence for the far-reaching influence of Corinth at this early time that the inhabitants of this distant valley should summon her artists to decorate their shrine.

The colours used are black, dark red, brown, orange and white, laid on flat without any attempt at shading, and to us, for whom sacred buildings are usually associated with grey stone and dark ivy, it is difficult to get used to the idea of so much colour on the outside of a temple, but one must remember that anything but the richest colours look dull and faded in the glow and light of a Greek hillside.

The painted clay metope, shewn here in Fig. 1 a, is a primitive piece of work, but would serve its purpose vividly. The single figure, drawn in outline and filled in with colour, stands out boldly, and the artist wisely has not tried to crowd further incident into the one frame, already shewing the Greek love of drawing the human form clear and unobscured by accessory detail. Fragments of another metope shew that the pursuing Gorgons were on a second panel. A third was decorated with the monstrous bearded Gorgoneion shewn in Fig. 1 b.

Perseus hurries right, "at full stretch", a rather clumsy, angular figure, with long legs and a disproportionately small torso. Notice that the torso is in front view while the legs are in profile. A primitive artist does not draw so much what he sees as what he knows is there, and this kind of mental vision always sees things in their most characteristic outline—legs in profile, torso frontal and eyes in full, even in a profile head. The problem of drawing the torso in profile needs some power to suggest the third dimension and is beyond the grasp of the early artist; for a long time this continues to be the conventional way of drawing the body.

He wears the cap of darkness and winged shoes; the *harpe*, a long,

1a

1b

straight sword, is in its scabbard, slung over his shoulder; under his arm he carries the head of Medusa, half-hidden in the *kibisis*, or bag. This head is drawn in a surprisingly human fashion and is in striking contrast with the grotesque Medusa heads of other early Greek representations.

Though Perseus is bearded this does not make him old. It was the archaic fashion to let the beard grow, even for young men; only after the middle of the sixth century are the younger gods and heroes shewn clean-shaven (cf. Fig. 12). His dress is just the usual Greek chiton, a sleeveless tunic, made all in one piece, though, being coloured yellow and brown above and black and brown below, it is made to look like two garments. It clings close to the body without any appearance of being separate from it, for it is not until nearly a hundred years later that the Greek artist learns to draw the folds of drapery at all realistically.

FIGURE 2. A PAINTED CLAY RELIEF found in Syracuse. Second half of the seventh century B.C. (ht. 56 cm.)

ANOTHER very decorative piece of work in coloured clay comes from Syracuse, and the fact that Syracuse was a colony from Corinth may have had something to do with the artist's choice and treatment of his subject, which seems to have been a favourite one with Corinthian artists (cf. Fig. 7). The relief is richly coloured, red, black and cream. It may perhaps have been one of the two acroteria that stood out against the sky, set up over the lateral corners of the pediment on the archaic temple of Athena. Though fragmentary, there can be no mistake as to how it should be restored (the white parts in the photograph are the modern plaster restorations). The winged Gorgon figure is deliberately worked up into a formal, stylised design, the lines of the face, especially, making an elaborate bit of pattern-work.

The chiton and boots are red, richly decorated; the wing-feathers are red and black, outlined with cream; the pupil of the eye is black inside a red circle.

Tucked in under the Gorgon's right arm is a small Pegasos, the winged horse that sprang from her blood when she was beheaded by Perseus. The artist, happily able to disregard the real order of events, pictures him here, beside his mother before she is slain.

The exaggerated action of the arms and the curious, kneeling attitude of the legs are early artistic conventions to express the speed of figures rapidly running (cf. Figs. 4 and 5, though notice that Fig. 1 a, in spite of its early date, has a more natural treatment of the legs).

It is exceptional at this early period to find the Gorgon running from right to left (cf. Fig. 18); the reason for this change perhaps is that it is really one of a pair of balancing figures, where it would be necessary for one of them to be reversed.

2

3 a

3 b

FIGURES 3 *a* and *b*. A CLAY PITHOS[1] WITH DECORATION IN RELIEF. Louvre, CA 795. Boeotian, second half of the seventh century B.C. (ht. 1·30 m.)

AT first sight this design in relief, with a curious horse-bodied woman, does not seem to have much connection with the story. But the man is most certainly Perseus; his conspicuous hat and the *kibisis* hanging from his left shoulder have been modelled with elaborate care and give the clue, though his boots have not the wings that Hesiod speaks of (do not mistake for wings the curling tongues of leather at the top of the long boot; this is the usual fashion of the period). And we are left in no doubt about the identity of the hero when he is so clearly shewn turning his head well away from the monster he slays, as the legend says Perseus did for fear he should look on Medusa's fatal countenance. Notice the shape of his sword, the *harpe*; only on early vases is it shewn as a straight blade, as here, where it seems to be a long one-edged knife; on vases of a later period it is shaped more like a sickle (cf. Figs. 14, 16, etc.).

There is no legend to explain this strange Medusa with the body of a horse, but one must remember that the horse Pegasos sprang from her blood, and the people of Boeotia, where this vase was made, seem to have clung to many queer, primitive stories about half-human monsters and men and women changed into beasts; and it may be that some local legend about a Medusa, half-woman, half-horse, lingered on among the people, known to the village potter though it never appeared in the poet's version of the story which the Boeotian Hesiod gives us.

The face of Medusa seems to us no more terrible than that of Perseus; the addition of the two rows of enormous teeth is the

[1] For explanations of the Greek vase-names cf. the Glossary, p. 98.

most that the potter could do to express her awfulness. There are no snakes or wings. Notice how the pattern of wavy lines that decorates the dress is carried on over the horse's body. The small salamander is put in the field to the right purely for decoration; it is similarly used on other Greek vases. The early Greek artist had a horror of leaving any large empty space in his design.

The relief is modelled free on the neck of a large pithos of reddish clay, which was found at Thebes and probably had stood above a tomb. Though the scene seems grotesque in our eyes, the work is very skilfully done in a difficult medium and is a sincere effort to picture the glory of the great hero's deed—a noble monument to set above a man's grave.

FIGURES 4 *a* and *b*. A BLACK-FIGURE BOWL in Berlin, 1682 (diam. 55 cm.). FIGURES 5 *a* and *b*. A BLACK-FIGURE NECK-AMPHORA in Athens, National Museum, 657 (ht. 1·22 m.). Attic, late seventh century B.C.

(The background is the reddish, buff colour of the clay; the grey parts in the photograph represent the purple paint.)

T HOUGH ARGOS claimed Perseus as its local hero, his picturesque legend was common property, and we find the potters of many different cities making use of it to decorate their vases. Here (Figs. 4 *a* and *b*) is the earliest Athenian version, and it gives us an interesting example of local patriotism, for Perseus, who originally had nothing to do with Athens, is shewn watched and protected by Athena, the city's guardian goddess. There is no mention of her in Hesiod's version of the story, but it seems that, at an early date, Athenian artists saw to it that she had a share in the great hero's adventures, and she continues to play an important part in the story.

We would not recognise the later warrior maiden (cf. Fig. 8) in this quiet, cloaked figure, were her name not written clear beside her—*Athenaia*. The traces of a leg and foot at the broken edge of the fragment probably belong to Hermes, god of travel and adventure, another new protector who is also henceforth incorporated in pictures of the legend.

Perseus (he is labelled *Pereus*, which seems to be an Attic version of his name, the letters running from right to left according to the earlier system of writing) is a businesslike figure, with *harpe* and *kibisis* slung round him and the cap of darkness tied firmly under his chin. His sandals have wings and he moves from left to right, as is the rule with all the figures in these earlier examples. Notice the profile legs with the frontal body and again (cf. Fig. 2) the archaic "kneel-running" attitude. Hesiod must have had something of the sort in mind when he wrote: "His feet did not touch the shield and yet were not far from it—very marvellous to remark, since he was not supported anywhere" (cf. p. 9).

Early Attic vase-painters before this had given their designs an ill-defined and rather dazzling effect by using a mixture of styles, some parts rendered in dark silhouette, other parts in outline drawing, and often with the addition of patches of purple and white, while all the space not occupied by the main design was dotted over with little filling ornaments. But now, by the end of the seventh century, they are beginning to learn how weak, on the curved side of a vase, is a thin outline drawing and how boldly the solid silhouetted figure stands out on the light clay. We shall see this silhouette method, the so-called "black-figure", carried to perfection later when the contrast of well-balanced light and dark masses is used to its full value. Here the method is still in the experimental stage. The figure of Perseus is in black-figure— a silhouette with the inner details drawn on the black glaze with some fine incising tool (it seems very probable that this peculiar and difficult technique is derived from bronze-engraving, which was a well-developed art at an early time in Greek history) and with a lavish use of purple paint laid over the black for chiton, cap and shoes (and face!). But the old outline drawing is still used in the figure of Athena, with the face and arms left in the colour of the clay. This conventional way of contrasting the fair skin of the woman with the dark, sunburnt skin of the man is often followed later, even after the use of outline is abandoned, by laying white paint over the black silhouette (cf. Figs. 8 and 14).

The background is still strewn with little patterns; it is a long time before the Greek artist can bear to leave blank the spaces in his design. Drapery is either flat like a board or drawn tightly

4 a

4 b

5 a

5 b

round the body, there is still no attempt to indicate the folds. Notice the differentiation between the fierce male and the gentle female eye: Perseus's is round, Athena's almond-shaped—a system that continues right through the Attic black-figure style. Gorgons and other monsters have the round, male eye.

From the fragments of the vase that remain (Fig. 4 b shews the vase restored) it seems doubtful whether the artist ever completed the scene with the figures of the Gorgons. But luckily he put them on another vase which has been recognised as his work, the famous "Nessos" vase—so called from the picture of Heracles slaying the Centaur, Nessos, which decorates the neck.

Here (Figs. 5 a and b), on the body of the vase, are Medusa and her sisters, but, strangely enough, the other actors in the scene are omitted. The figures are all in silhouette with dress and details in purple laid over the black (as half-human monsters, the Gorgons do not qualify for the pale flesh of other female figures). They have high curved wings which seem to be incorporated in a curious way with the front of the dress and they speed along in the same "kneel-running" pose as Perseus on the Berlin bowl. Medusa sinks to the ground with folded wings, the blood spurting from her neck; with her left hand she clasps her knee as she falls. Again there is much space-filling ornament, even a stray bird is brought in to fill the gap left above the fallen Medusa. The dolphins below are not simply a decorative frieze; they serve also to suggest "the springs of Ocean" where Perseus found the Gorgons sleeping.

There is something very grim in the way the horrible creatures prance in step with measured strides across the surface of the vase, as though in some hideous dance of death. Damaged and patched as the vase is, one feels how the artist, with little power yet to observe and reproduce natural appearances, and working mainly from a mental picture, with the limbs of the figures stiffly bent and their actions crude, has nevertheless been able to express all he wanted in the bold, symbolic way in which he presents the subject.

The vase was found in the Kerameikos, the cemetery of ancient Athens; it stands four feet high, and, like the vase in Fig. 3, was used as a tomb monument. It was made to be seen from the one aspect only, facing those who stood before the tomb; its decoration is all on the one face, the other being covered with a plain wash of black glaze, and it is this economy of work that must account for the curious absence from the scene of the chief character, Perseus, with his helpers, Athena and Hermes.

FIGURES 6 *a*, *b* and *c*.   A BLACK-FIGURE LEBES (BOWL)
AND STAND in the Louvre, E 874.   Attic, early sixth century B.C.
(total ht. 93 cm.)

THIS vase, the whole thing measuring over a yard high, a magnificent example of what can be done on the potter's wheel, is slightly later in date than the last and shews the black-figure technique fully developed: all the figures are in silhouette with the inner details incised: there is no line drawing and the filling ornament is gone. But the artist has no idea yet of the great possibilities that lie before him. The design has not the broad swing of the two earlier examples and the figures are lifeless and uninspired in comparison. Here is the whole company— Perseus is in flight with the two deathless Gorgons, Sthenno and Euryale, after him, a grotesque little Medusa sinks to the ground and Athena and Hermes (with his *kerykeion* or herald's staff in his hand) look on. The flesh of Athena is black as in the other figures. The Gorgons have snakes in their hair and high-curved wings that now spring from the back, a less clumsy arrangement than the one used by the artist of the "Nessos" vase, and, instead of the old "kneel-running" convention, they have a more natural pose, with both feet on the ground.

On the other side of the vase (Fig. 6 *b*) are two warriors fighting, each with his four-horse chariot behind him; they have no connection with the main scene.

The rest of the vase and stand is cut up into decorative bands; the animal friezes are dull and mechanical, a queer jumble of elongated lions, lionesses, boars and goats and men and Sirens. They are the stock patterns that are found on a whole series of Attic vases made about this time, an idea perhaps derived in the first place from the rows of beasts that are so frequent on oriental works of art. Greece was in contact with the East and, from a much earlier time than this, her artists would be influenced by the rich oriental fabrics, textiles, embroideries and metal-work, that would reach her market. But such purely formal decoration cannot satisfy the restless genius of the Greek artist, and he soon learns to put his own vital spirit into the new technique which he has perfected. The fine palmette and lotus decoration is also of eastern origin; it is a favourite Egyptian motive and reaches the Attic artist via Corinth, where, for many years, the vase-painters have been at work refining and elaborating it.

6 a

6 b

6 c

7 a

7 b

THE chance finding of a sculptured block of stone led, in 1911, to the discovery of an archaic Doric temple near the town of Corfu. Though the temple itself was much destroyed, most of the sculptured slabs of the west pediment were found in a wonderfully undamaged state. This enormous Gorgon, measuring over nine feet high, was the central figure of the composition. On her left is a male figure on a much smaller scale who must be her son Chrysaor; on her right are traces of the wings and body of a small Pegasos; beyond, on either side, is a great crouching lion, and, towards the angles of the gable, are figures representing the battle of the gods and giants. (Fig. 7 b gives a conjectural restoration of the pediment.)

Comparison with vase-paintings shews that the work is Corinthian in style. Corcyra was a Corinthian colony (cf. Fig. 2) and, though the citizens seem to have been always on bad terms with the mother-city, this would not prevent them getting first-class workmanship from Corinth for the decoration of their temple, and even if the sculptors were actually Corcyreans, their traditions and style would be under Corinthian influence.

It may seem odd that this uncouth, grimacing figure should be given the place of honour on the temple pediment, but the idea behind it takes us back to a time long before these Gorgon-figures were identified with the creatures of the Perseus legend.

With her attendant lions, she embodies the great Nature Spirit of primitive belief who appears in early Asiatic and Ionian works of art as a goddess with birds, lions or snakes heraldically set on either side of her, the prototype of the Cybele of Phrygian worship and the Artemis of the Greeks. Here, through one aspect of her nature, she has become partly identified with Medusa, the mortal maiden of legend, with her offspring, Chrysaor and Pegasos, beside her, though she is not yet linked up with her slayer, Perseus. The group shews one stage in the making of a myth and throws light on the complexity of ideas that have been gradually absorbed and welded together to make the finished, coherent story.

It must have made a magnificent decorative motive in the centre of the triangular pedimental space. The work is clumsy and angular in design, cut out in such high relief as to be almost in the round, though surfaces are flat and modelled only hesitatingly. But the artist has made up for his lack of skill in modelling by the delicate pattern-work he has put into the details of the hair, the chiton, the boots and the magnificent snake girdle. Other snakes coil themselves behind her and in her hair.

There are only fragments of the finely worked wings left. The head is hideous with great bulging eyes and wide-open mouth; the protruding tongue and the beard have been broken.

Faint traces of paint are still to be seen, and it is probable that the whole figure, with the background and the architectural setting, was brightly coloured. It is difficult to realise that colour played such an important part in Greek sculpture when we are used to seeing galleries of statues in the pale marble, but the custom was general, and in earlier works, certainly in those made of coarser stone, the surface seems to have been completely covered with a coat of paint.

THE florid style of this kylix seems to be a protest against the growing importance of the severe black silhouette technique. All the drapery is purple, white is used wherever possible and, above and below the figure frieze, the artist has crammed in elaborate decorative bands.

Here again is Perseus's flight from the Gorgons. It is curious that the earlier artists choose this for their subject rather than the actual beheading of Medusa, which is not frequent in Greek art until some time later (Figs. 13, 15). One would perhaps have expected the more concrete, graphic scene to have appealed to the earlier artist's range of ideas.

To the left of the scene is the body of Medusa, and the birth of the horse Pegasos is crudely pictured by setting a horse's head on her shoulders. (The design here is only faintly to be seen, lightly traced on the clay ground of the vase where the paint has flaked away.) The addition is grotesque and luckily does not take its place among the details that become traditional in pictures of the story.

Perseus hurries off to the right, gay in a white hat and dappled fawn-skin; the *kibisis* and *harpe* are just visible behind him. Hermes follows and Athena comes lumbering along, rather hampered by the six great snakes that spring from the fringe of her aegis. This is a new conception of her; instead of the peaceful, cloaked goddess, she is now the armed warrior maiden with spear and shield. There is some approach to profile drawing of the torso in the way the curved breast is distinguished from the straight back. The two small nude male figures shew the same. Athena's flesh is no longer shewn in the old outline technique, but to emphasise the fairness of her skin, white paint is now laid over the black (cf. Fig. 4).

The two avenging Gorgons are in pursuit. The artist's love of white paint has allowed them the white flesh of female figures. They have huge snakes twined round them and trailing on the ground. They have the old, high-curved wings attached behind, but there is a new type of wing now coming into fashion, straight and like a bird's, and the artist gives them both.

It has been suggested that one of the small standing male figures is Chrysaor, who, according to the legend, was born with Pegasos from the blood of the slain Medusa, but perhaps, like the other male figure set beneath the handle of the vase, this is only a "spectator". Similar figures, male and female, often occur on early vases. They have no part in the action and have been added by the artist in his anxiety to leave no space in his design unfilled.

8 *a*

8 *b*

9 a

9 b

IN this early black-figure period we find a number of Attic vases with scenes more or less on the lines of Figs. 6 and 8. The artists devoutly follow the tradition as it has been handed to them and the subject is in danger of becoming stereotyped.

Suddenly Corinth produces a daring genius who finds a quite new and unexplored side of the story—the rescue of Andromeda—and makes his own version of the subject. Its strong pictorial effect reminds us that Corinth in the seventh and sixth centuries was a famous centre of painting.

It is a lively scene and every detail of the fight is put in with naïve delight. The hero and heroine are just two cheerful young mortals such as might be seen any day, flinging stones in self-defence at some fierce shepherd dog in the fields around Corinth. Perseus, nude, with a pile of stones at his feet and one in each hand, bravely faces the monster; Andromeda (the lower part of her body has been broken away), behind him, all eager help, has both hands full of stones ready for him. (An early French archaeologist takes them to be buns!) This is a peculiar rendering of the story; later artists shew Perseus attacking the monster with the *harpe*, and in some literary versions he petrifies it by holding up the Gorgon's head (cf. p. 14).

The figures have their names beside them—even *Ketos*, "the monster"—written in the Corinthian form of the Greek alphabet.

Notice the distinctive treatment for the female figure—the almond-shaped eye and the flesh drawn in outline and filled in with white to make it stand out from the clay colour of the vase.

It shews rather an advanced power of artistic selection that only

43

the head of the monster appears; early art, as a rule, seeks to tell the whole story and put everything in at whatever cost to the design. Three waves of dark paint below are enough to give the setting; to a Greek eye, a more elaborate landscape would only obscure the action of the picture.

It is disappointing that this spirited version of the story was never, as far as we know, followed up. The vase was found in a tomb at Caere in Etruria—perhaps it was shipped away by some clever trader before the Greek world had had time to admire and imitate it. Andromeda does not appear again in pictures of the legend until a much later period and then she is tamed and grown up and has a much less exciting part to play (cf. Figs. 29–33).

PERSEUS and the Gorgon sisters are here set on the panels which decorate the three feet of a finely made round clay casket. The pictures follow closely the Attic tradition and need little comment. Perseus (Fig. 10 *c*) is labelled, the letters running from right to left. He has hat, winged shoes and *kibisis*, but no *harpe*. On separate panels are the two Gorgons, and with the last (Fig. 10 *a*) is the body of Medusa, clasping her knee as she falls just as she does on the Attic vase, Fig. 5. Notice that the wings of the Gorgons are attached, in the same awkward way, to the front of the body. There is much purple used—for Perseus's chiton and shoes and for the Gorgons' faces and wings.

The lower halves of the three feet of the vase have pictures of a wrestling match, a boxing match and a disc-thrower with an umpire watching the throw.

With the three panels of the Medusa story, I figure also a piece of the frieze that runs round the side of the vase, a picture of five dancers and a flute-player. The technique is borrowed from Attic black-figure work, but the spirit is typically Boeotian. The Boeotians were always made fun of by the more urbane Athenians for their stupidity and dullness and their enormous appetites; the saying "Boeotian swine" was an ancient Greek proverb. But, from this vase, one can imagine that there was a lot of quiet village wit that the clever "foreigner" was never allowed to see. There is the real genius of caricature in the contrast between these absurd little figures and their exalted gestures.

It often happens that pictures of an old-established story are hampered by traditional renderings of it and the artist cannot give full play to his imagination (for who was ever popular who introduced variations into a favourite fairy-tale?). This is apparent in the vase shewn here. The pictures of the Medusa story, well guarded by popular tradition, shew little originality or freedom; only in the dancing figures, where he need not follow an established tradition, can the artist really let himself go.

In view of the local connection, it is interesting to find that four of the scenes on this vase—the Medusa story, a festival, a wrestling bout and a hare hunt (the last not figured here)—appear also grouped together among the subjects figured on the shield in the Boeotian poem, Hesiod's *Shield of Heracles* (ll. 216–304), cf. p. 9.

10a 10b 10c

10d

10e

11a   11b

11c

A BLACK-FIGURE LEKYTHOS in Paris, Bibliothèque Nationale, 277. Attic, middle of the sixth century B.C. (ht. 14·8 cm.)

THIS lovely little squat oil-jug, only about six inches high, is a good specimen of the fine craftsmanship of the middle of the sixth century; style, shape and design all seem to be so exactly suited to one another. There is a lot of delicate incision; purple is carefully added over the black to lighten dress, wings, shoes and other details and, painted directly on the clay, it makes a more vivid colour for the blood that drips from the *kibisis* and from Medusa's neck. White is used on the dresses for a fine border pattern of small dots. The artist is now beginning to think more in terms of design; instead of having all the figures hurrying to the right as has been the rule hitherto, he gets a simple kind of cross-rhythm by turning three of them in the opposite direction, and for the first time there seems to be a rudimentary idea of linking the figures more closely together as a group instead of treating each as an isolated unit.

Medusa falls to the left with pretty, drooping wings; Athena and Hermes face the pursuers with upraised hands, as though to protect Perseus. The same variety of direction is used in the frieze on the shoulder of the vase. (Notice the little "spectator" figures that fill the spaces between the horsemen: cf. Fig. 8.)

Athena is now the warrior goddess, fully armed with helmet, snake-fringed aegis and spear, and stands stiff and straight like some archaic temple statue.

FIGURES 12 *a* and *b*. A BLACK-FIGURE AMPHORA in the British Museum, B155. Chalcidian, middle of the sixth century B.C. (ht. 48 cm.)

THE so-called "Chalcidian" vases form an important group, distinguished by definite characteristics from other black-figure vases, yet there is still a mystery as to their place of origin. The chief reason for attributing them to Chalcis, in the island of Euboea, is that the alphabet used in the inscriptions on many of them has the local peculiarities of the Chalcidian alphabet, and, in a more general way, the style of the vases, though it is closely linked with the fabrics of the Greek mainland—especially Corinth—shews characteristics such as one might expect from the people of Chalcis, which was originally a settlement of Ionian Greeks from Attica and was famous for its bronze-work, as its name, Chalcis, "city of bronze", implies. Unfortunately sherds of this kind of pottery obstinately refuse to turn up in any excavations in Euboea, while it is very doubtful whether any of the vases now in museums were found in Greece, and the fact that nearly all the vases come from excavations in Italy has led to the suggestion that they were made by Chalcidian workmen who had migrated west. It is difficult to believe that if they had been made in Greece and carried to western markets, no trace of their manufacture would be found on Greek soil. The problem is full of difficulties, to be solved one day perhaps by the spade of some lucky excavator.

The vase shewn here has all the fineness of technique that is a mark of the group. The clay is a rich, deep orange-red, the glaze even and a good black and the shape is well defined and has almost the clean-cut effect of metal-work. The design is simple, with no overlapping of the figures, and its rich rounded lines are perfectly suited to the curves of the surface of the pot. The artist has a feeling

48

12 a

12 b

for form and style that is still strong enough to control his gifts of naturalistic drawing and keep them within the bounds of the technique he is using.

On one side (Fig. 12 b) is the picture of Heracles's fight with the triple-bodied Geryon. On the other side is a lovely scene: Perseus, wearing a purple chlamys and with the *harpo* at his side, clean-shaven, as is now the fashion among the young men of Greece, stands with hands upraised in delight and surprise while the three river-nymphs, the Naiads (their name here is written in the Ionic form, *Neides*), like three stately cypresses, stand before him, each bringing her gift—winged shoes, hat of darkness and the *kibisis*, decorated with tassels and spots of purple: "A bag of silver—a marvel to see—and from the bag bright tassels of gold hung down." Athena stands beside Perseus, unarmed, with her purple himation (cloak) drawn over her head. Under their himatia, the Naiads wear the Doric peplos, a dress made of a heavy piece of cloth folded round the body and fastened with pins on the shoulder; here, as often, the top, with its embroidered border, is folded over and allowed to hang loose. On the himation of the middle figure of the three (the head and the upper part of the body have been restored) we at last find an elementary rendering of the folds—slightly curved incised lines running parallel and diagonally across the figure. The other drapery in the picture still remains flat and unwrinkled. Notice how the dress of the leading Naiad clings closely to the contours of her back and legs; this is a characteristic of Ionian drawing.

FIGURES 13 *a* and *b*. A BLACK-FIGURE JUG in the British Museum, B471. Attic, middle of the sixth century B.C. By Amasis (ht. 26 cm.)

(Fig. 13 *a* reproduces the design only in outline. The figures are really all black. The hatching represents the purple paint.)

GREEK vases were never the mechanical products of a factory and the artist's signature that we find on many of them is evidence for the pride that the individual craftsman took in his work.

The signature *Amasis mepoiesen* ("Amasis made me") appears on this vase and on seven others, and the artist's style is individual enough to be recognisable on over forty other unsigned vases or fragments. The Egyptian name, Amasis, suggests that the man may have been foreign born, perhaps one of the foreign *metics* who contributed so much to Athenian industrial supremacy.

He abandons the old hard-worked motive of the pursuit and chooses the moment just before the death of Medusa. She tries to flee from Perseus, but he has caught hold of her and, with head averted, plunges the *harpe* into her neck. The Gorgon type is more elaborate; she wears a fawn-skin fastened at the waist by two knotted snakes and small snakes writhe round her head; she has both types of wing, the curved and the straight. Perseus is beardless; his *kibisis* is a curious great loose sack, and he wears a fawn-skin and a chiton embroidered with stars and with the border embroidered and fringed.

All three figures shew a more careful study of anatomy and proportion. In Perseus we still see the old difficulty in drawing the shoulder of a figure viewed in profile, though in Hermes, cloaked and less active, the effect is more successful.

On other vases signed by Amasis we find a new power of

13 *a*

13 *b*

observation in the rendering of drapery; it is disappointing that this example of his work is not so adventurous and shews the dress, as do other earlier vases, flat and without folds.

We have now come to a new phase in vase-painting. The early artist drew his pictures almost as symbols to express his ideas, with figures set in certain poses that vividly conveyed his meaning, though the actions were crude and often bore little relation to nature, for he had not yet learnt to observe and copy appearances accurately and still worked largely from the mental picture which he had formed.[1] At a later stage we shall see the artist with much greater power to reproduce things as they appear, a gift that is to prove as dangerous as the proverbial three wishes; it gets beyond his control and nothing can undo the mischief of its working.

In Amasis we have an interesting between stage; he clearly can reproduce things more nearly as he sees them (one must compare his other work[2] to realise fully the new skill in naturalistic drawing that he brings to the art), but his mind is absorbed in the arrangement and the setting of his figures and he deliberately keeps them rigid and stylised and subordinate to his carefully planned design.

He cuts down the long, loosely knit frieze of figures and concentrates his subject to one episode, and by this limitation he intensifies the interest in the composition. It is the formal pattern that his picture makes that holds his attention, the two men symmetrically placed on either side of the Gorgon whose lines—wings, limbs and snakes—all radiate starlike from the centre. The disposition of the various kinds of surface is carefully planned too, the plain black equally with the fine decoration—fringed

[1] Compare a similar "symbolic" motive that is common even now—the horse racing with all its four legs outstretched, like a rocking-horse. Photography has proved that a horse is never in such a position, yet the motive so vividly conveys the idea of a horse going at full speed that it is still in use.

[2] On p. 97 I give a list of other works by Amasis in the British Museum.

cloaks, spotted fawn-skins and chitons edged and spotted with purple. He knows exactly how far he can go within the bounds of the black-figure technique and uses all its strange power to the utmost. The clay has the glowing, orange-red tinge that Attic potters have now learnt to give to it; the black glaze is smooth and even and has a wonderful depth of tone and the incised lines have a lovely delicacy and sweeping precision.

So much finely incised decoration closely set in certain places almost alters the surface texture of the glaze and makes it look like chased metal-work, though one must see the vase to realise it; the drawing does not reproduce the effect. This, with the sharply defined contour of the vase-shape, its grooved handle and finely turned lip, makes one wonder if the artist could have learnt this technical perfection as a worker in bronze.

HERE we have reached a much more advanced stage in representation. With a more naturalistic treatment of the figures, gestures are less angular and there are new devices for dealing with the complexities of the folds of drapery—the mass is broken up by a number of incised lines which come down to meet the uneven, zigzag line of the hem. Fine waving lines are used to suggest the thinner texture of Athena's long chiton. There is an entirely new feeling in the work, and there was something new in Athens to account for it—the invention of the red-figure technique (cf. Fig. 16), which opened up fresh fields of possibilities to the vase-painter. The grace and freedom of this new method are reflected in the contemporary black-figure work, breaking down the boundaries of stylistic convention that were really essential to the true nature of the old technique. It is a sign of the times that the graceful figure of Athena takes the central place, her shield on the ground beside her; Medusa's dead body is too gross and has to go. Notice the slight introduction of landscape—the dark mass of the mountains that lie below Perseus in his flight with a long, ribbony tree growing out of them, a queer, conventional symbol, certainly not based on the direct observation of nature. A line of white, outlining the mountains, means snow on the tops. Landscape never plays a big part in Greek painting; when it is introduced at all, it is of the simplest and only used as a setting, quite subordinate to the human figures which are always the chief interest.

For the first time Perseus carries the new form of *harpe*, the curved, sickle-like blade that appears always on vases of the red-figure style. Hermes is an elegant figure such as any well-dressed

Athenian of the time might be, wearing a quaint, pointed hat and with his hair looped up in the S-shaped knot known as the *krobylos*.

The artist has tried to soften and refine the Gorgon sisters on the other side of the vase and, by making them more nearly human, has succeeded in turning out something more horrible than the quite unreal, imaginary bogeys of earlier black-figure art. Their flesh is painted white, like Athena's, over the black silhouette. Their dress, the long Ionic chiton, is new and reflects a change in the fashion of the time, for, about the years 540–530 B.C., Attic women gave up wearing the long Doric peplos which they had worn up to that time—a heavy piece of material folded round the body and fastened by large pins on the shoulder (cf. Fig. 12)—and took to the more graceful Ionic chiton which was made of a finer material and sewn on the shoulder to make a little sleeve. This new dress probably came in with other eastern luxuries under the influence of Pisistratus; only after the Persian wars, on the wave of a new national consciousness, does the Dorian dress come back into fashion (cf. Fig. 24). The Gorgons here wear the long chiton knotted up round the waist to give them freedom. Snakes rear up above their heads; the leader has the new bird's wings alone, the other keeps the older, high-curved type as well.

14a   14b

15a

15b

15c

FIGURES 15 *a*, *b* and *c*. A LIMESTONE METOPE IN HIGH
RELIEF, from Temple C at Selinus. In the Museum at Palermo.
End of the sixth century B.C. (ht. 1·47 m.)

SELINUS was a colony founded by Greeks during the seventh
century B.C. on the south coast of Sicily, and it was her
quarrel with her neighbour Segesta that led to Athenian
intervention in Sicilian affairs and the fatal expedition against
Syracuse. At the end of the fifth century the quarrel was revived
and Selinus was sacked by the Carthaginians. Earthquakes have
since completed the work of destruction. The city was planned on
an immense scale and the ruins of it, on a low hill close to the
seashore, are very impressive; the giant fallen blocks lie piled up
in tumbled heaps everywhere all among sand and tamarisk and
thickets of aromatic bushes. Eight temples of the Doric order have
been identified, nearly all of them built on the same lavish scale.
They are distinguished prosaically by letters of the alphabet. One
of them, known as Temple G, has columns over eleven feet in
diameter. Fig. 15 c shews the fallen monolithic columns of
Temple C. The metopes that decorated the frieze of this temple
are now in the Museum at Palermo; Fig. 15 b shews how they
were set, with alternating groups of triglyphs, below the cornice,
the usual system on temples of the Doric order. The three best-
preserved metopes represent a four-horse chariot in full-face,
Perseus beheading Medusa and Heracles carrying the impudent
little Kerkopes fastened upside down to a long pole.

At first sight one would date this Medusa metope about a
hundred years earlier; in fact, until a short time ago, it was so
dated. There is no particular design or any attempt to fill the
metope artistically, the figures are just set in a row, all turned to
the right, the last figure, Athena, very much cramped for space.

55

It is a clumsy piece of work, done by a backward provincial sculptor who has been able to copy a few little up-to-date mannerisms in the details of his work, such as the folds of Perseus's chiton and of Athena's peplos, which are treated in a way which is not found on vases till late in the sixth century. But the actual figures seem very primitive; they are awkward and badly proportioned—though something in the way they are cut and the strong modelling of the big muscles makes them alive and interesting.

Head and body are in full-face, legs and feet in profile—Athena's feet are strangely twisted. The limbs are heavy and thick-set and the heads too big, with huge, flat eyes and projecting ears. The figures have been cut out in very high relief so that they stand out almost as statues in the round, but they have not been cut back to a uniform depth and the background is at all sorts of uneven levels.

As usual on a Greek temple, figures and background, like the stone of the building itself, were all brightly coloured. Traces of the paint can still be seen.

ABOUT the year 525 B.C. comes the new technique—the red-figure—and the old black-figure method gradually dies out. Instead of the more limited black silhouette with incision, the figures are now left in the colour of the clay against a background of black, and the inner markings are shewn by thin lines of black or brown paint. Added white and purple are seldom used, they are no longer needed to lighten and vary the dark silhouettes of the design. Crude conventions, such as the distinguishing of the sexes by colour or the shape of the eye, are now abandoned. It is a much easier means of expression and naturally allows of much freer drawing. At first the vase-painters do not know how to make full use of it and for some years they still follow the conventions of the black-figure style, as is natural when, as it often happened, the one artist worked in both styles—sometimes even using both on one vase. But by the first years of the fifth century they have already begun to realise the possibilities of the new method. Many of these artists' names are known to us from the signatures on their vases, and there are besides many whose individuality can be just as clearly recognised through their work though they have left no name. By a minute study of the style and detail in the drawings archaeologists have been able to group together whole series of vases as the work of individual artists and, for purposes of study and identification, have given each artist a name invented from some characteristic piece of work.

One of them has been called the "Berlin painter" from his masterpiece in the Berlin Museum, which shews a wonderful grouping of three superimposed figures with an effect of depth and space that would have been impossible in the old black-figure technique. The design shewn here is not so enterprising; it is still haunted by the need of making a strong contour and the figures are drawn flat, with little attempt to shew roundness or perspective, but they are strikingly decorative, set, one alone, on either side of the vase, straight on to the black ground of the big amphora, which stands nearly two feet high.

The early artist, still struggling with the practical difficulties of making it clear what his picture is about, and following with reverence each detail of the sacred story, must put in every character who plays a part in the scene, and the black-figure representations of the Perseus legend, nearly all of them with the same number of figures, become rather monotonous. But now the red-figure artist loses interest in the actual narrative and it becomes for him only the grand quarry where he may find the material to suit his artistic needs. The Berlin painter loves especially to set a single figure only on each side of his vase (cf. the vases by him, or of his school, in the British Museum, E 266, E 267, E 268, E 269), so here he takes only Perseus and one of the Gorgon sisters; Athena, Hermes and even Medusa herself must go for the sake of the artistic effect.

The drawing still follows the established tradition, with the figures moving from left to right, but the position of the legs is more convincing and more natural than the black-figure "kneel-running" convention. The pursuing Gorgon has the conventionalised, hideous mask and Perseus is bearded in the archaic fashion, but now the Gorgon wears the long Ionic chiton, instead of the short one that she always wears on archaic black-figure vases, and Perseus carries the new curved type of *harpe*. In spite of the archaic setting, there is a new feeling for drawing and the flow of a line in the Gorgon's crinkly dress and in the waving folds of Perseus's chiton: for the curved line is the natural product of the

16*a*

16*b*

16*c*

brush while the straight line was characteristic of work done with the incising tool, and yet, even with this new freedom, the artist still loves to stylise his drawing and he groups the waving lines of Perseus's chiton into a pattern of palmettes. Though the gestures are conventional, arms rigid and fingers spread, and the decorative purpose comes first, one can see the new interest in the human body and problems of form, and the struggle to make the figures live that came with the discovery of the red-figure style; the clothes, too, hang more naturally and seem to be more a part of the wearer. The Gorgon's himation (cloak) swings out as she runs; contrast with this the straight, hanging folds of the Gorgon's dress in Fig. 14. Notice the careful study of the muscles, which can be more freely rendered by the painted line than by the old, rigid method of incision, and how the lines of the eye in Perseus's profile head are left open at the inner end and the pupil set nearer to the inner corner, making it more lifelike and expressive. The incised line is no longer used, and where a dark part of the design, such as Perseus's hair and beard or parts of the Gorgon's wings, comes against the black ground of the vase, the outline is shewn by a thin line reserved in the red clay. The Gorgon's dress is a little confusing: she wears a himation, folded and fastened on the shoulder, as it is worn on many of the marble statues of Athenian maidens in the Acropolis Museum, and under it, actually, a single long Ionic chiton, but the artist has a fondness for decoration and especially for scattering surfaces with small stars and dots, and here he has patterned the smooth stuff of the skirt while leaving plain the finely pleated neck and sleeves, which gives the effect of there being two garments. (He does the same with the dress of a goddess on another vase, a krater in the British Museum, E468.) Like Perseus, the Gorgon wears a *nebris*—the skin of a fawn or panther —the end of it is just visible below the himation.

FIGURES 17 *a* and *b*. A RED-FIGURE KALYX-KRATER in Leningrad, 637. Attic, early fifth century B.C. By the Triptolemos painter (ht. 41 cm.)

EVEN in the early years of the fifth century a new spirit can be seen in the Greek vase-painter's treatment of mythological subjects. The well-worn theme of the killing of Medusa is typical of the older mentality, striving to make a vivid, narrative picture and frankly enjoying the grotesque ugliness and every realistic detail. Then comes a change, the horrible Gorgon of the Perseus legend goes out of favour, it is too uncouth for the Greek's new sensitiveness to beauty, and the painter turns instead to the lovely pathos of Danae's story.

He is no longer occupied only with the action of a scene but seeks instead to shew the effects of the action on the thoughts and feelings of the individual figures—a quieter, subtler art.

One side of this vase shews Danae—her name is written beside her—in her prison, visited by Zeus in a shower of gold; she is unwinding the long fillet that binds her hair, when suddenly she stops and gazes upward, inspired by the revelation of the great god's presence. The artist has done all he can to make the scene rich and delicate: the supports of the bed are carved and painted, the pillow and mattress elaborately decorated: there is a feeling for the texture of the stuff in the fine folds of Danae's chiton contrasting with the heavy sweep of her woollen himation. Simply with a mirror and embroidered head-dress (a *kekryphalos*—the drawing on this page shews one of the many ways in which it may be worn) he cleverly suggests the setting, and they are quite enough to make us feel the reality of the wall on which they hang.

17a

17b

On the other side of the vase Danae is already in the chest that is to be her floating prison and Acrisios stands by to see his decree carried out. The cramping line of the open lid is awkward, but it is forgotten in the beauty of the central figure, Danae holding the child in the crook of her left arm, while with the right she makes a final gesture, perhaps refusing to yield and to deny her story of the divine parentage of her son; the artist has lavished fine work upon the details of her hair and diadem. Perseus is shewn as a well-grown boy,[1] for, as we see so often in primitive pictures of the Madonna and Child, the early artist can only picture a child as a miniature man. His hair is neatly rolled up over a fillet that is fastened in a loop at the back of his head; he lies, quietly holding his ball in one hand.

To the left of the picture is the carpenter, intent upon his work, drilling holes in the edge of the chest for clamping down the great lid. His tool, a bow-drill, is carefully drawn; he presses down the thick, short drill firmly with the left hand while with the right he pushes backward and forward a long bow, and the string of the bow, passing round the drill, makes it revolve.

The name of Acrisios is written on the black ground beside him; it was a common practice, both on black- and red-figure vases, to write their names beside the figures in this way; the letters have also a decorative value and perhaps the earlier artist's dread of a blank space in his design still lingered on.

The phrase written beside the carpenter, *ho pais kalos*, "the boy is fair", has no reference to the scene and arises in another way. The Greek vase-painter, especially in the red-figure period, would sometimes write on his vase the name of a youth, perhaps some young nobleman or athlete who was a popular favourite in Athens

[1] According to Pherecydes's version (p. 5), Perseus was three or four years old when he was discovered by Acrisios.

at the time, with the word *kalos* after it—*Megakles kalos* or *Miltiades kalos* (we find famous names among them)—this would give his wares an extra appeal to the eye of the public, just as enterprising salesmen of to-day offer us Marina blue or Mickey Mouse tooth-brushes, and, at any rate, he would secure one good customer when next a krater and kylikes were needed for a banquet. The phrase has many variations but often it appears, as it does here, simply as *ho pais kalos* without any dedicatory name.

The painter of this vase is unknown, but his individual style has been recognised. Notice his love of fine work in the drawing of the accessories—Danae's dress, the bed, the tools, and, on the chest, the actual markings of the grain of the wood and the three holes bored in the side to let the air pass in. Notice too the use of white paint for old Acrisios's hair and beard and the realistic fall of the hem and folds of his heavy cloak with the small weights fastened to the corners to make it hang in place. Yet the artist has skill enough to keep the detail subordinate to his main design—the rich central figure, framed and emphasised by the simpler flanking figures, and there is something new in the way the lines of the body of the carpenter, in three-quarter view, give an effect of space and make the figure stand out in the round, no longer an outline on a flat plane.

Is it fanciful to see in the two pictures a definite balance of design?—the Danae picture based on a triangle, upside down, with the apex at her feet; the carpenter picture, also a triangle, but upright, the apex in Danae's head with her shoulder and the lid of the chest carrying up the lines of the two sloping sides? A man who draws tools as carefully as this would not be one to let his designs develop haphazard, he would be more likely to work out some ingenious way of setting them in the framework of a balanced geometric figure, delighting in the problem of working out the decorative value of ordinary everyday things.

18 *a*

18 *b*

THE artist has been given this name because the great god Pan, pursuing a shepherd, is the subject of one of his most brilliant pictures. About eighty vases and fragments have been identified as his work. His drawing has all the strength and ability of the artists of his time and there is an unmistakable suggestion of a third dimension in the twist of the bodies of Perseus and Medusa, but, with it, he delights in a kind of deliberate quaintness that is apt to distract from the real charm and brilliance of his work. The figures here seem to be dancing in some exquisite Russian ballet, with their posturing and elaborate arm movements. Athena, with delicately lifted skirt, trips along after a prancing, exuberant Perseus; Medusa falls dead on tapering, posed fingers. Once more she wears the short chiton; red-purple paint is used for the blood that pours from her neck. There is a lively feeling for detail in the varieties of drapery, in the sweep of the wings on Perseus's hat and boots and in the gruesome little saw-edged *harpe* with its elegant spiral handle. (Notice that it has the new curved blade.)

The sloping line of Athena's spear seems to carry the eye down to the sinking figure of Medusa, then there is a sudden upward spring, up towards Perseus's raised right hand, that gives a feeling of swift movement away to the left and out into the air.

Now, for the first time, the direction of the picture is reversed and the figures move from right to left; it is curious how this new plan of design is adopted by all the later red-figure artists while the left to right arrangement was the only one used by black-figure artists.

It is a further break with the old tradition to shew Perseus without a beard and the half-hidden head of Medusa is no longer a hideous mask, and her snakes are gone.

FIGURE 19. A WHITE-GROUND LEKYTHOS in the New York Metropolitan Museum, 06,1070. Attic, first quarter of the fifth century B.C. (ht. 25·7 cm.)

BESIDE the black-figure on a red ground and the red-figure on a black ground, the Attic vase-painter used a third method—covering the surface of the vase with a white slip before painting his design on it. There are difficulties with the slip, to get it smooth and white and to make it stick firmly to the clay, and these white-ground vases were always more perishable and liable to flake and could never have been in common use. Indeed the greater number of them seem to have been made solely as funerary offerings, to be used only once, to hold perfumes and oils at the tombs of the dead. It is interesting to speculate what the Greek vase rooms in our museums would be like if white china clay had been known to the ancient Greek potter.

At first the black-figure artists set their dark silhouettes on this white ground, then they realise that the light ground offers quite a new possibility: on it an outline can be made with a single line to stand clear and strong, when it would be lost if left to stand alone on the ordinary dark clay. So a new technique begins, that of a simple outline drawing, but it is not until later, with the further discovery of the effect of a thin colour wash for parts of the design (cf. Fig. 24), that we get an independent style and technique properly suited to one another; the beginnings are experimental and follow the conventions that rule the more familiar black- and red-figure designs.

This lekythos is an interesting example of the transitional stage, a combination of the black-figure and outline methods. The artist still loves to see a good black silhouette on his vase and Perseus is thus shewn, black, with incised inner markings and with plenty

64

19

of the red-purple paint that usually accompanies black-figure work; it is used for *kibisis*, boots and the wide-brimmed hat that is perched at a dangerous angle as apparently young Greeks liked to wear it. But one might almost guess that the artist has been looking at the red-figure hydria of Fig. 18: a black-figure Perseus running left is unexpected: he has a curved *harpe* and it is in his left hand: the head of Medusa is just visible over the top of the *kibisis*—these are all red-figure innovations. The figure of Medusa, too, seems reminiscent of the same design, twisted and half-fallen, though with wings of the high-curved type used by the earlier black-figure artists (cf. Fig. 8)—and here is the new technique with the fine-drawn outline shewing clear on the white surface of the vase. We go back again to black-figure for the winged Pegasos that rises from her neck. There are sham inscriptions in the field.

The lekythos has a sharply curved side which makes it unsuitable for a number of figures set in close relation to one another and it really needs a special form of composition to suit the narrow field. But the artist has chosen a subject that has grown up on, and become adapted to, the wider surfaces of the more usual black- and red-figure vase-shapes—hydriai, amphore and kylikes; he seems to have just cut out the main figures from some larger design, without considering the slim, upward lines of the vase.

FIGURE 20. A RED-FIGURE LEKYTHOS in the Museum of the Rhode Island School of Design, Providence, 25·084. Attic, second quarter of the fifth century B.C. (ht. 14 cm.)

THIS little drawing, with the sea-birds, lightly sketched and impressionistic, fluttering round Danae and Perseus, strikes quite a new note and gives a strangely un-Greek feeling of atmosphere and the setting of nature. It makes one wonder how far Simonides's poem (p. 11) could have reached the people of Athens for the vase has something of the same lyrical spirit, quite outside the usual range of the Greek potter. The artist's method of drawing is original too; he makes a light panel on the side of the vase with the open lid of the chest and against this the figures are drawn in outline.

20

21 *a*

21 *b*

FIGURES 21 *a* and *b*. THE LID OF A BLACK-FIGURE PYXIS
in the Louvre, CA 2588. Attic, second quarter of the fifth century B.C.
(diam. 13 cm.)

BY the beginning of the fifth century B.C. all the finest Attic
vase-painting was in the red-figure style, but the black-figure
lived on, even far into the fourth century, though without
its early vigour. The example shewn here is an interesting mixture
of the new and the old schools. With the black-figure technique,
the artist uses a subject that was only popular with black-figure
artists—the pursuit of Perseus by the Gorgons—but with all sorts
of changes—not always for the better—that shew the influence of
the red-figure treatment of the legend. The painting is careless and
the incised lines in many places do not follow the lines of the glaze,
but there is a grace and lightness of touch that give the picture a
charm though it has lost the strength of design and brilliance of
technique that were really the essence of black-figure. Notice that
the figures move from right to left, a system that is not usual until
the red-figure period.

The subject is a black-figure one, but it is treated with the
red-figure artist's freedom. In the sixth century the artist looked
on the story he was painting as a sacred thing and his skill was
devoted to painting it worthily, but later the story becomes entirely subordinate to his artistic purpose and details are treated
with less understanding and reverence. Here the artist has un-
imaginatively repeated the same type of figure for all three Gorgons,
which means that Medusa, though headless, is running at full speed
with arms outstretched. No other black-figure artist shews such
a heartless lack of imagination; in all other black-figure versions
of the scene, Medusa is decently allowed to sink to the ground
beneath the stroke, but the grim legend means nothing to the

painter of this pyxis lid; it merely provides him with a number of swift little figures for his design, and Medusa must run with the rest.

She has the early up-curved wings, but instead of the short peplos which she wears as a rule in black-figure work, she wears here a long billowing chiton with a deep pouch at the waist caught up by a girdle of snakes, clearly derived from the early red-figure conception of her. The lines of her wing-feathers are hastily scratched on and go straying out on to the background beyond the paint. On either side of her, smaller than the other actors in the scene, are the winged horse Pegasos and a male figure that can only be Chrysaor. The two rows of dots in the field seem to be a kind of sham inscription; perhaps the artist is working from an original that was inscribed and has been too lazy or too ignorant to copy the actual letters.

The two sister Gorgons are also transformed; their heads are human and in profile and they wear long chitons like Medusa's. The first one holds up a clumsy little bit of drapery in one hand, the line of her other arm has flaked away.

Hermes heads the flight, wrapped in his chlamys and wearing long boots with a flapping tongue in front and a curious kind of hat; he has not got his usual *kerykeion*, but both he and Perseus carry a couple of spears and Athena carries another.

The spear does not appear in early black-figure drawings of the subject; it is the red-figure artist's addition to the story. We find it first in Athena's hand in the late black-figure example, Fig. 14, and after this it is often introduced into pictures of the legend, though in quieter scenes where it is not so incongruous. Here the artist has fastened upon the spear and multiplied it for his artistic purposes, quite regardless of the needs of the story. The long lines are effective and give a sweep to the design, but two heavy spears

68

would not be much help in beheading Medusa (the *harpe* is forgotten) and would make flight a decidedly difficult matter. After Hermes comes Perseus, running with great strides—notice that he and Hermes are really running, it is not just the "kneel-running" pose of the earlier black-figure drawings; his boots are like Hermes's and without wings; he has his cap and his *kibisis* with Medusa's head just visible.

Perseus is followed by an Athena so tall that there is no room for the crest of her helmet; she has a spear and on her outstretched right arm waves the aegis, fringed with lumpy little snakes. She races after Perseus and Hermes—they are like three conspirators— but it is her last frolic; after this a new spirit of repose takes the place of adventure and action in the artistic conception of the story; the later fifth century prefers its gods to behave with a proper dignity. The design is really delightful and there is a light-hearted swing about the figures that is further enhanced by the circular setting, which seems to carry the eye with it and add to the sense of whirl and flutter—but how angry it would make an artist of the old school to see his legend treated so lightly and ignorantly and his fine glaze so rough and blurred!

FIGURE 22. A CLAY RELIEF. Berlin, 8382. Melian, second quarter of the fifth century B.C. (ht. 17 cm.)

IN all the wealth of Attic art, we must not forget that there were local schools of art in other parts of Greece, though, it is true, they come more and more under the influence of Athens as time goes on. These Melian reliefs, of which there are over a hundred, have been found on various sites, several of them on the island of Melos, and probability points to their having all been made there within a short space of time, approximately between the years 475 and 440 B.C. They have a character of their own and they represent in a rich and picturesque way many scenes from Greek legends that are not so usual in Greek art, some of them with marked literary association—Orestes and Electra at the tomb of Agamemnon, Odysseus and Penelope, and Nereids with the arms of Achilles (British Museum specimens shew, among others, Eos carrying off Kephalos, Helle on the ram and the death of Actaion, cf. the list on p. 97). We cannot trace the origin of their style; there are no early beginnings, and the earliest of them are not really very far behind the latest in development. It must just have been some new turn of fashion that suddenly created a demand for these reliefs, when they were exported as far as South Italy and the Troad, and then, just as quickly as it sprang up, the little local industry dies out.

The reliefs were made by pressing the soft clay into moulds, the same mould being in many cases used more than once. (The subject given here is repeated in one in the British Museum, B 365, which is less perfectly preserved.) They were coloured, red, blue and yellow, and, being pierced, could easily be fastened on to wooden panels and were in all probability used to decorate the sides of caskets, providing a cheaper form of decoration when

22

carving in wood or ivory or metal repoussé would be beyond the means of the ordinary citizen. The colour on this specimen has perished.

Medusa, in a long chiton, is fallen on her knees, her arms held out in a gesture of helplessness, and her right leg trails along the ground—the old "kneel-running" pose transformed beyond recognition. A small Chrysaor springs from her neck with arms outstretched to the left. Above her is Perseus, riding a horse, with a small conventional Gorgon mask in one hand and the *harpe* in the other (the reins would also be in this hand, but, being added in colour on the surface of the clay, they have disappeared). His body is turned slightly from the full front view and his head is turned right over his shoulder—why, I do not know—perhaps looking at the pursuing Gorgon sisters, perhaps just because he is so often shewn in this position, with head averted as he slays Medusa.

But why is Perseus riding? There is the idea of Pegasos, of course, always in the story, but never do we hear of Perseus mounting him. The explanation of this is not mythological but artistic and is found in another relief of similar type (B.M. B 364) which shews Bellerophon, mounted as Perseus is here, on Pegasos (wingless also) with the Chimera below him in the place of Medusa. The artist needed a balancing group and, with the thought of Pegasos lurking in his mind, has used him to make Perseus a mounted figure too.

FIGURE 23. FRAGMENTS OF A RED-FIGURE KRATER in the British Museum, E493. Attic, middle of the fifth century B.C. By the Villa Giulia painter (ht. of fragment about 30 cm.)

A LOVELY krater in the Villa Giulia in Rome gives this artist his name, but I fear that this fragmentary painting gives little idea of the charm of his work, though I figure it here because it shews so well the changes that are coming over the art of the vase-painter. No longer need he struggle to make his figures live, he is master of his craft and can represent what he chooses without effort; he can give effects of depth and roundness; the drawing is supple and easy; details have been reduced to the essentials and there is a nobility in the figures, calm and aloof, that reminds one of the contemporary sculptures of Olympia. It is the detached and untroubled beauty of the classical period in Greek art. The effect of the whole vase when unbroken must have been monumental.

The eye is now drawn carefully with eyelid and lashes and in correct side view.

The scene shews well how the artist's approach to his subject is changing. It is as though the Greeks had suddenly grown up, their spirit awakened by the great ordeals of Salamis and Plataea. In the sixth century it was the action that held his imagination, Perseus beheading Medusa or already in flight, pursued by the avenging sisters; now, with a more subtle sensibility, he chooses the moment of suspense that is the prelude to the drama.

Perseus, his hair hanging loose and treated in a new and informal way (notice the contrast with the neatly dressed hair of Fig. 18), stoops with averted head over the sleeping Medusa; on either side of him are Athena and Hermes, tranquil and dignified. The fastening of Athena's cloak is interesting: here, actually in use, is

23

one of those enormous pins that are often found on classical sites and seem so impossibly clumsy and awkward to fix. Another krater by the same artist, B.M. E492, has a lovely picture of Hermes dandling the baby Dionysos and shews him again in this attractive hat.

On the ground lies a strange Medusa, a good example of the Greek fifth-century artist's lack of a "sense of ugliness"; he cannot help giving her a body lovely and supple in its soft, clinging dress, and all he can do to suggest the monstrous is to give her a head of negroid type, merely pathetic in its plainness—the tusks and tongue are far from convincing. It is a contrast with the black-figure artist's frank enjoyment of his grinning, grotesque inventions.

FIGURES 24 *a* and *b*. A WHITE-GROUND PYXIS in the Louvre, L 83. Attic, middle of the fifth century B.C. (ht. 14·8 cm.)

THIS circular pyxis has a scene like the last, but in the rarer technique, with the surface of the vase first covered with a white slip before the design is painted on it. This shews the later development of the method that was used for the lekythos of Fig. 19, but the black silhouette is now gone and, on the outline figures, whole surfaces are filled with a dull colour-wash. The colours are simple, just different depths of a dull purple. The art is moving out along new lines and has become practically painting in the modern sense of the word, with new effects of light and shade that never came within the scope of the black- and red-figure methods.

It is not a finely finished piece of work, for the delicate white slip can only take a quick, firm sketch, but the figures are gracefully set to decorate the sides of the box and there is a flowerlike freshness and simplicity about it all that we only find in these small white-ground vases. The majesty of gods and hero is forgotten, and the scene has the friendliness of some little *genre* painting that suits well with the intimate nature of the purpose of the vase— to hold a lady's trinkets.

The design is much like the last, only in a reverse position. Perseus, with head averted, approaches the sleeping Medusa, who lies in a rocky hollow underneath a naturalistic tree; her head is again of negro type but no longer made hideous with fangs and lolling tongue.

New characters in the scene are Poseidon, the lover of Medusa, and a Gorgon sister who sleeps beside her. The heavy stuff of Athena's peplos falls in soft natural folds, a contrast to the formal, patterned folds of the Gorgon's dress in Fig. 16.

24 a

24 b

The vase belongs to a time when the great masters of painting were making amazing advances in their art. The famous wall-paintings of Polygnotos must have been seen and discussed by every Athenian craftsman, and many a vase-painter must have gazed, intoxicated, at the free brushwork and the shading colours of these huge pictures and perhaps gone home with his head filled with dangerously ambitious plans.

The white ground of these vases would encourage imitation of the wall-paintings, and this may partly account for the sketchy, broad treatment of the figures and the use of naturalistic landscape on this pyxis, though, certainly, the composition is kept well within the scope of the vase and there is none of the heavy grandeur that we might expect if it were closely modelled on one of the larger paintings. The Greek artist had no shame in borrowing a good design when he saw it; if he saw good material he must use it too and see what his own genius could make of it. Originality was not so rare at this time in the world's history that there was any need of copyright, but there was no slavish copying and the vase-painter's personal style coloured and transformed everything he borrowed.

Besides the two examples given here in Figs. 23 and 24, there are four other adaptations of the same subject on vases, which rather suggests that there was some famous contemporary wall-painting in the background, though there is no literary record of such a picture.

FIGURE 25. A FRAGMENT OF A RED-FIGURE KRATER in Oxford, 1917·62. Attic, third quarter of the fifth century B.C. By the Kleio painter (ht. 10·5 cm.)

HERE we return to the story of Danae. Danae and her child are in the chest while Acrisios stands by, relentless, his spirit symbolised by his rigid staff that towers above his daughter's bowed head.

In contrast to the earlier vases, one feels, even in such a fragment as this, the new spirit that has come into the artist's treatment of his figures, bringing a new stateliness of pose and a new ethical grandeur—the spirit that finds fuller expression in the sculptures of Pheidias. The quiet dignity of Danae—she is a king's daughter and wears a fine diadem and delicate veil—conveys all the tragedy of her story without any strained or theatrical gesture.

Notice how a greater intensity of feeling is now put into the drawing of the eyes; the way in which young Perseus gazes directly at Acrisios makes a link between the figures on either side of the separating space that earlier artists could not give with their less perfect means of expression.

25

26a

26b

26c

FIGURES 26 *a*, *b* and *c*. A RED-FIGURE BELL-KRATER in Bologna, 325. Attic, third quarter of the fifth century B.C. By the Polydectes painter (ht. 21·5 cm.)

THIS vase is of the same period as the last, but already seems to have something self-conscious and theatrical about it. The subject is new: Perseus, with two spears, stands in the centre of the picture holding up the Gorgon's head and gazes at Polydectes as he slowly turns to stone. Polydectes, a bald old man, holds out a beseeching hand as he feels the change come over him; from the waist down he is already stone. Athena in a new and dramatic pose, her foot resting on a rock, looks on, aloof and unmoved. White paint is once more coming into use to give brilliance and variety to the design. Her arms and face are painted white and the Medusa head is painted too, but it is disappointing that the paint has flaked so, for it seems that here the artist has abandoned the old tradition, making it the head of a lovely mourning woman. This is the first example we have had of a human face in front view, for up till now we have seen only the Gorgon mask so drawn. It is not indeed the first example in Greek vase-painting, for even in the early days of black-figure Greek artists wrestled with the problem of how to draw the head in front view; still, the technical difficulty was enough to make frontal heads a rare occurrence on vases before the middle of the fifth century.

The other side of the vase gives a continuation of the scene, a youth, with his cloak wrapped about him so that it covers the lower part of his face, gazes at a warrior, half-hidden by his great shield—one of Polydectes's followers who has already become a pillar of stone.

The artist has clearly no longer any difficulty in representing the third dimension; the figures are almost sculptural in the way they stand out from the surface of the vase. The different planes of Athena's figure are cleverly suggested and Perseus's figure, with a supple twist of the body and the feet so easily drawn in front view, might almost have been planned as a statue in the round. But one has a feeling that the game has now become too easy and the artist seems rather to parade his skill, the flesh is so soft and the lines so fine and flexible.

It is worth while to pause a little and compare this vase with some of those of a hundred years earlier, to see how the technique and vision of the artist have changed—and more than this, how the whole mentality of the Athenian people must have changed too. They have ceased to respond to the great tale of the young hero's deeds; they demand something that will stir a deeper sensitiveness; the tension of a dramatic moment takes the place of the earlier, slow unrolling of epic narrative. It is not what men do, but what they think and feel that now interests them and the artist must have the skill to shew them the minds and spiritual reactions at work in his characters.

With the sculptures of Pheidias, the paintings of Polygnotos and the plays of Sophocles constantly before his eyes, it is no wonder if the Athenian citizen lost his head a little among all this grandeur and majesty and expected to find it everywhere. In this clever world there is no place for the vase-painter. His little art breaks under the demands put upon it. His technical skill remains superb, but he abuses it. He has acquired a wonderful new power of expression, but this very power is soon to prove the ruin of his art. Evidently drawing much of its inspiration from the great wall-paintings and panel-pictures of the period (Pausanias[1] saw, in the Propylaea, a picture of "Perseus, on his way back to Seriphos, carrying the head of Medusa to Polydectes" which may have some

[1] Cf. p. 16.

78

connection with the picture on this vase), his subject-matter is too rich for the old medium; its freedom has no relation to the surface of a vase and ignores the limitations naturally set to a work of art carried out in line drawing with black glaze upon red clay. On vases of the archaic period the figures were essentially decorative and the pattern of their lines enhanced the lovely lines of the pot on which they were drawn, making a beautiful thing of it. Design and technique were one. Now the pot is forgotten, the artist begins to treat it more as a painter treats his canvas, and, with his mastery of perspective, with subtle twists of the figure and surging draperies, he carries the eye back into space, behind the surface of the vase, interrupting shape and unity.

For a little time the vase-painter holds himself in check and some lovely things are still produced, but the fourth century brings a loosening of restraint and there is a riot of florid, showy work, a lesson in misdirected skill.

FIGURES 27 *a* and *b*. THE LID OF A RED-FIGURE PYXIS in Athens, National Museum, 1956. Attic, late fifth century B.C. (diam. 18 cm.)
(The reproduction does not give the black background of the design.)

THE subject is a new one—Perseus's visit to the Graiae, or Phorkides. According to Pherecydes's version of the story, cf. p. 6, Perseus stole their one eye, refusing to give it back until they should tell him the way to the Nymphs who had the magic sandals, cap and *kibisis*. The artist seems to have had his own ideas about the appearance of the Graiae, "sisters grey from their birth", and has shewn them as young dark-haired maidens, but notice that he has not forgotten their blindness, the eyesocket of each is drawn in but there is no eyeball. One of the sisters holds the tooth in her outstretched hand and Perseus creeps up between the other two, ready to seize the eye as it passes from one to the other. He already wears winged cap and sandals, which may imply some different version of the story, or more probably the artist has given him his usual attributes thus early to make his identification sure. He is loaded with two unnecessary spears and the *harpe* hangs in its sheath at his side.

Hermes and Athena, the hero's guardian spirits, are here—and with them are two new characters, old Phorcus, who was the father of the Gorgons and of the Phorkides, and Poseidon, the lover of Medusa. Leaping dolphins remind us that the scene lies "beyond Ocean".

There are fragments of a play of Aeschylos, the *Phorkides*, and it is possible that this sudden venture outside the traditional material of vase-painting is inspired by it.

The dignity of the heroic subject seems to have gone and instead there is a feeling of superficial prettiness that we have not had till

80

27a

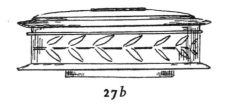

27b

now. The design is somehow mechanical and one does not feel the spirit of the artist alive in it; it has no underlying plan to link the figures together, they turn this way and that but seem curiously dead and separated from one another. They seem to be just stock figures grouped together without any feeling for the story—what is Athena doing, hurrying along with lowered spear in her right hand while she still holds her great helmet in the left?—and sceptres, trident and spears make ugly cross-lines that break up the sweep of the circular setting and divide the scene into meaningless pairs of figures.

FIGURES 28 *a* and *b*. A RED-FIGURE HYDRIA in the British Museum, F500. South Italian, late fourth century B.C. (ht. 26·9 cm.)

AFTER the Syracusan disaster at the end of the fifth century the Athenians were no longer able to keep up their export trade in the west and this led to an enormous increase in the output of the local potteries in the Greek cities of Southern Italy. For many years before this the Athenian workshops had supplied these western colonies, but we find also plenty of local work to shew that there must have been a number of potters in Italy who had learnt to imitate the Attic work. But there is always a tendency to exaggerate in size and design and to make a showy effect with touches of added colour—yellow, white and purple—and the black varnish loses its fine, dark lustre. Now, when the old standards are lost, this mixture of a decadent Greek with a coarse native culture was not a good material for an artistic revival, though the results were not always as poor as the example shewn here.

A mincing little Perseus tiptoes away with the head of Medusa, whose body stays, seated elegant and erect. At the end of the fifth century the *harpe* takes on this new form—a mixture of dagger and sickle (cf. Figs. 30 and 31). The artist, clearly ignorant of the old legend, has confused the pursuing Gorgon with a figure more familiar to him, the winged Victory which is a common art type— only that he has omitted the wreath which she usually carries.[1] The great head that rises out of the ground to the left of the picture is one of the stock designs of the Italian vase-painter and is constantly used in this grotesque way to fill up a vacant space. On the shoulder of the vase is a Gorgon's head worked into a decorative scroll.

[1] Fig. 28 *c* shews the reverse of an early fifth-century coin of Syracuse, a Victory crowning the horses of a victorious chariot.

28 a

28 b

28 c

SO far we have only had one picture dealing with the story of Andromeda (Fig. 9), and even there her romance plays only a small part and the chief interest centres round the fight with the monster. But now, in the second half of the fifth century, under the influence of famous stage representations, Andromeda's side of the story becomes much more popular with the vase-painter than any other, though, with the intrusion of ideas borrowed from the drama, the continuity of the vase-painter's tradition is broken.

There are a number of vases that seem based on some kind of dramatic setting; three of them are reproduced here. We know that both Sophocles and Euripides produced plays on the subject, but we must not expect to find in these vase-paintings any direct evidence for the actual staging of their plays. The vase-painter has to treat his subject freely, for his picture must speak for itself and must give a general impression of the play rather than reproduce any one isolated moment on the stage.

The binding of Andromeda is pictured in various ways; on some vases, curiously, she is shewn bound to pillars or tree-trunks, a version so unlike the traditional story that we may suppose it to be based on the very simple and limited setting of the Greek stage, when the columns that stood at the back of the stage often did duty as scenery. (On one late vase she is actually shewn sitting fastened to an ornate chair!) Where she appears bound to a rock, one may perhaps see the influence of the more realistic stage effects of the Euripidean stage.

FIGURES 29 *a*, *b* and *c*. A RED-FIGURE HYDRIA in the British Museum, E 169. Attic, third quarter of the fifth century B.C. (ht. 45·6 cm.)

THIS is surely a stage scene and the suggestion has been made that it is inspired by the play of Sophocles which was produced in the year 442 B.C. The details of the scene are puzzling and we have no clue to the curious setting. Ethiopian slaves are busy setting up the pillars to which Andromeda is to be fastened; the tall figure, supported by two more slaves and wearing what is the usual Amazon dress with long sleeves and tight-fitting trousers under a short chiton, must be Andromeda herself, though there is no explanation of her dress beyond the fact that, like the Amazons, her home is in the East. Slaves bring articles of toilet, perfume-jars, mirror, stool, casket and cloak, as funerary-bridal gifts in accordance with the Greek belief that the maiden who died unwed became the bride of Hades in the underworld.

Cepheus sits by, sunk in grief, a most dramatic figure; both he and Andromeda wear the high cap of oriental royalty. Perseus, still invisible, stands behind him with his hand to his forehead in a gesture of horror and pity.

The reproduction given here can hardly do justice to the delicacy of the work and the omission of the dark background takes away a lot of the rich effect of the vase. There is some lovely drawing; the figure of Cepheus, especially, is beautifully done. The artist is quite at his ease in shewing many of the figures, and the face of Andromeda too, in front view.

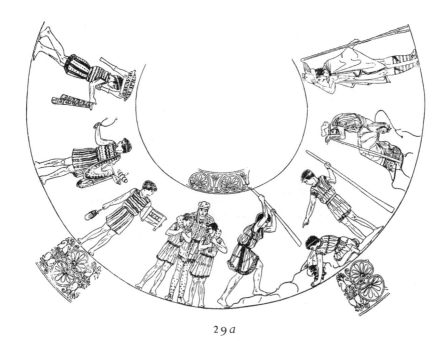

29a

29b

29c

30a

30b

A later moment of the story is shewn here. Andromeda is now bound, awaiting her doom, and Perseus has come and stands before her. Instead of the pillars, it is a naturalistic rock to which Andromeda is fastened, indicated by faint white lines and the little plants and sprays of flowers that spring out of it. Andromeda wears a richly embroidered dress and a tall Phrygian cap; above and below are three bridal chests. On either side of her are Cepheus and Perseus; beside Cepheus stands Hermes with his *kerykeion*, and beside Perseus stands Aphrodite, crowning him with a garland. An Ethiopian maiden (probably a member of the Chorus) sits on one side; on the other side is a burning altar. The composition now becomes more elaborate and is treated more like a free painting, and an effect of distance is given to some of the figures by setting them at a higher level or by partly obscuring them behind a contour of the landscape.

We cannot hope to find on this vase a reproduction of any actual dramatic episode; the presence of so many characters at once upon the scene alone makes this unlikely, but it must be closely connected with some stage representation. The long dress worn by Andromeda seems to be a regular stage costume. On a krater of the same date in the Museum at Naples (3240), which shews a group of actors, one of the figures wears just such a robe as this, with the same decoration of horses' heads embroidered on the breast, the spirals on the sleeves and the deep rays on the hem.

A stage scene would also account for the altar to the right of the picture; it has nothing to do with the story, it is a part of the artist's memory of the play, the great altar of Dionysos which stood in the orchestra and was the centre of the sacred ritual of the Attic theatre.

Euripides's *Andromeda* was first performed in the year 412 B.C., and one may reasonably believe that this vase, which was painted soon after that date, is an echo of the excitement it caused in Athens. The play was a famous one and, from the fragments and records we have of it, it seems that the poet struck a new note in the pure and romantic way in which he treated the love-story of Perseus and Andromeda.

Lucian tells a good story of the people of Abdera, all stage-struck. "Their favourite recitation was the *Andromeda* of Euripides; one after another would go through the great speech of Perseus; the whole place was full of pale ghosts, vociferating,

O Love, who lord'st it over Gods and men,

and the rest of it. This continued for some time, till the coming of winter put an end to their madness with a sharp frost."[1]

We do not know whether Aphrodite actually appeared in the play or not, but her presence here, in the place of Athena, the constant companion of Perseus through all his adventures, is significant and suggests that she appeared as *dea ex machina* at the end of the play, personifying this dominant love-note of the piece.

It is rather a startling thing to find that this is the first appearance of the love-romance on the Greek stage. The world has indeed grown up since the sixth-century artist painted his cheerful—and anything but love-lorn—couple as we saw them in Fig. 9.

[1] Lucian, *De conscr. hist.* I. 1, 2.

31

THE artist has surpassed himself. Besides an elaborate scene of sacrifice, with Andromeda standing on a stool and fastened to two tree-trunks, we have the great fight between Perseus and the monster; Eros flies down to crown the hero (for Andromeda's sake one is glad to think that her rescuer must remove his hat before he can be visible). Nereids are on either side.

There is no reason to suppose that the fight was ever actually shewn on the stage any more than the procession of sea-beasts that winds round the middle of the vase, but there is no knowing what might happen in the city that could produce such a vase as this, for, at a time when Greek plays were so popular in the Greek cities of South Italy, and when every city of importance had its own theatre and performances, one can imagine that the people's love of luxury and display might sometimes lead to elaborate stage effects of this sort.

As a comment on the history of "taste", one should note that it was vases of this decadent type that were the great pride of the wealthy collectors of the early nineteenth century, before scientific excavation had revealed the true origin of the art and the beauty of the Greek work of the earlier periods.

FIGURE 32. A POMPEIAN WALL-PAINTING. Naples, Museo Nazionale. First century A.D. Probably after a picture by Nikias, an Athenian of the second half of the fourth century B.C. (ht. 1·06 m.)

W E are apt to think of Greek art as sculpture first and foremost, but it is only due to the accident of preservation that sculpture takes such a prominent place. In the eyes of the Greeks their painting, from what we read, must have been just as great an art and actually, in their writings, there is much more said about their pictures than about their statues. But it can mean nothing to us when we have no originals or even credible copies of their great masterpieces. There are only a few fragmentary remains of Greek painting of a poor quality and we have to rely on other sources to learn something about it. Vases tell us something of the tendencies of the art of the different periods, and some of them, in subject and arrangement, may reflect famous pictures of their time, but they are really only linear work and give no clue to what could be done in free painting— the effects of brushwork, the colour, light and shade and space-sense.

We have literary records of many famous paintings, and some of the descriptions given by ancient writers are detailed and sensitive, but no words can capture the real essence and greatness of a picture. We get most help from these Pompeian wall-paintings. Shortly before the destruction of Pompeii in A.D. 79 it became the fashion to decorate the walls of rooms with figure compositions dealing with mythological subjects, setting them almost to look like easel-paintings in a large space on the wall, surrounded by an elaborate and fantastic architectural frame. It is clear that many of these pictures are based on famous Greek originals, and they must reproduce, to some extent, their subject and composition,

88

though we cannot hope to find in paintings of this date much of the real quality of works of the fifth and fourth centuries B.C.

The wall-paintings were the work only of well-trained crafts-men, who would naturally work largely from the pattern-books of their trade, containing systems of decoration and reproductions of famous pieces that they would be able quickly to work up and adapt to the scheme of the room's decoration to suit the taste of the owner of the house. There would be no careful, archaeological copying of the old technique, and all the tricks of the trade of later years would be at their disposal. It leaves us little hope of getting in touch with the original work as the great artist first conceived it.

The picture reproduced here is one of several, all more or less alike, the same figures appearing also in sculpture, on a mosaic and on coins, and presumably all are based on one great original. And this can only be the picture which Pliny mentions as the work of Nikias, a famous Athenian artist of the late fourth century B.C.

We know a good deal about him. It was he who coloured the statues of Praxiteles (Greek sculpture was not left in the white stone as we see it to-day, cf. Figs. 7 and 15), and Praxiteles used to say, when he was asked which of his statues pleased him most, that the statues which Nikias had coloured were the finest of his works. Plutarch tells the absurd story that when Nikias was busy on his famous picture, the *Nekyia* ("The Underworld"), he became so absorbed in his work that he had to ask his slaves whether he had washed and breakfasted. He maintained that an artist should choose grand subjects, cavalry engagements and sea fights, and not fritter his skill away on little things like birds or flowers. He devoted special care to the painting of women and made a close study of light and shade and of plastic effects. Many of his pictures were brought to Rome; one of them, a picture of Hyacinth, which was captured at Alexandria, was especially admired by Augustus

89

and was afterwards dedicated in his temple—which gives us a glimpse of how the art of the different centuries links up. Here the figures stand out, dignified and simple, dominating the scene in accordance with the fundamental Greek view that through the human form alone can supreme beauty be apprehended. There is a statuesque grandeur which is unusual at this stage of Pompeian painting, and this may mean that the copyist is following the original rather more closely, keeping the sculptural quality that it must have had, with clear modelling of the contours, not obscured by scenery or accessories. The Gorgon's head and the *harpe* are insignificant and the dying monster is just visible behind Andromeda's rock.

Notice the old contrast of the male and the female figures—the looming dark rock throws into relief the fair flesh of Andromeda, while Perseus's dark limbs are outlined against the sea and sky, seen through the archway in the cliff. The posing of the figures, standing isolated in the simple setting of nature, perhaps shews the influence of the romantic spirit of Euripides's play (cf. Fig. 30). The picture as originally painted by Nikias may have been still nearer to that vase-painting in conception. The awkward pose of Andromeda's left arm is easily understood if, in the original picture, it was fastened to the rock; the copyist has actually painted the dark fetter on her wrist, but, in ignorance of its real meaning, he has shewn it detached as an armlet. There is an astonishing variety and richness in the colouring. Against the green of the distant sea Andromeda's cloak is violet and her dress a shimmering yellow; Perseus's cloak is a dark wine-red.

32

33

FIGURE 33. A MARBLE RELIEF. Capitoline Museum, Rome, 89. Roman, middle of the first century A.D. (ht. 1·55 m.)

HERE is the same motive adapted to make a Roman decorative panel. Perhaps it should not be included here, but Greece has now become a Roman province and it is probably the work of a Greek, using Greek models, though he is working in Italian marble and for a Roman patron. The Greek motive is transformed and made trivial by an over-emphasis on the sentiment and romance of the scene. Interest in the actual work and its fitness as a design is lost.

The arrangement of the figures owes much to the picture of Nikias, but the two figures are mere adaptations by a skilful hand of famous sculptural works. The Perseus is based on a fourth-century statue of Hermes that exists in a number of late copies and seems to have been the regular stand-by of the Graeco-Roman copyist. The figure of Andromeda is not so well adapted; it is a variant on the figure of a dancing Bacchante which is based on late fifth-century work of the type of the Nike Balustrade in Athens and has also been copied many times. The dancing step and the tossing draperies are not very suitable here.

The thing is badly put together. The figures have not originated in one mind and they remain separate and unrelated. The panel falls into two parts with an ugly space between them, though it is probable that the background was coloured, which would make it less blank and throw the figures out into prominence. Perseus, posing gracefully, the Gorgon's head held behind his back, helps Andromeda as she steps from her rock—she might be a *prima donna* stepping from the concert platform, the gestures are so purposeless, so consciously pretty. One feels that her chief thought must be deportment and how to negotiate the slippery monster at her feet.[1] There is such technical skill, such fluency and power to express—even though nothing more than this sweet sentiment (one finds some parallel in another Roman version of the subject, in Ovid's *Metamorphoses*, IV. 665 ff.)—and yet there is a strange deadness about the composition, a contrast with the throbbing earnestness of Greek works of the sixth and fifth centuries B.C.

[1] Cf. Lucian's description of the scene, p. 15.

LIST OF ABBREVIATIONS

Beazley, *Att. Vas.* Beazley, *Attische Vasenmaler des rotfigurigen Stils.*

B.S.A.   *Annual of the British School at Athens.*

Buschor.   Buschor, *Greek Vase Painting* (tr. Richards).

C.V.   *Corpus Vasorum Antiquorum.*

Greek Sculpture and Painting. Beazley and Ashmole, *Greek Sculpture and Painting.*

J.H.S.   *Journal of Hellenic Studies.*

Neugebauer.   Neugebauer, *Führer durch das Antiquarium* (Berlin). II. *Vasen.*

Payne.   Payne, *Necrocorinthia: a Study of Corinthian Art in the Archaic Period* (Oxford, Clarendon Press).

Perrot.   Perrot and Chipiez, *Histoire de l'art dans l'antiquité.*

Pfuhl.   Pfuhl, *Malerei und Zeichnung der Griechen.*

Richter.   Richter, *The Sculpture and Sculptors of the Greeks.*

Séchan.   Séchan, *Études sur la tragédie grecque.*

LIST OF REFERENCES TO THE ILLUSTRATIONS
AND TO SOME FURTHER PUBLICATIONS

Figure

1 a.   *Antike Denkmäler*, II, 51, 1.

1 b.   Payne, fig. 23 D.
        Cf. also Pfuhl, figs. 480–482; *B.S.A.* 1925-6, p. 124; Swindler, *Ancient Painting*, p. 120, Pl. VI.

2.   E. Douglas van Buren, *Archaic Fictile Revetments in Sicily and Magna Graecia*, Pl. XVIII, fig. 76 (John Murray).
        Cf. also Payne, p. 81.

3 a and b.   *Bulletin de Correspondance Hellénique*, 1898, Pls. V and IV.
        Cf. also Courby, *Les vases grecs à reliefs*, Pl. III, 2.

4 a.   *Archäologische Zeitung*, 1882, Pl. 9, 2 (Phot. Hellenic Soc. 363).

4 b.   Neugebauer, Pl. 8.
        Cf. also Perrot, X, figs. 66–69; *Archäologischer Anzeiger*, 1923–4, p. 46.

5 a.   *Antike Denkmäler*, I, 57. (Phot. Hellenic Soc. 3537).

5 b.   *Antike Denkmäler*, I, 57.
        Cf. also Pfuhl, figs. 85, 89; Buschor, Pl. XXIII; Beazley, *Attic Black-figure: a Sketch*, p. 10.

6 a.   E. Pottier, *Vases antiques du Louvre*, II, Pl. 62, 1 (Librairie Hachette).

6 b and c.   *C.V.* Louvre, fasc. 2, III Hd. Pls. 16, 2; 15, 2.
        Cf. also Payne, pp. 192, 346; Perrot, X, Pl. II.

7 a.   Zervos, *L'Art en Grèce*, Pl. 108 (Éditions Cahiers d'Art).

7 b.   *Cambridge Ancient History* (Vol. of Plates, I), p. 197, fig. b.
        Cf. also *Greek Sculpture and Painting*, fig. 28; Lawrence, *Classical Sculpture*, fig. 19; Richter, figs. 61, 76, 96, 109, 141, 374; *American Journal of Archaeology*, 1911, p. 349.

8 a.   *J.H.S.* 1884, Pl. 43.

8 b.   *C.V.* British Museum, fasc. 2, III He. Pl. 8, 1 c.
        Cf. also *Metropolitan Museum Studies*, V, p. 96, No. 62.

9 a.   *Monumenti Inediti dall' Instituto*, 1878, Pl. LII, 1 (Phot. Hellenic Soc. C 4796).

9 b.   Neugebauer, Pl. 13, 2.
        Cf. also Pfuhl, fig. 190; Payne, p. 110.

10 a–e.   Phot. Treue, Berlin.
        Cf. also *Archäologische Zeitung*, 1881, p. 29; Neugebauer, Pl. 9.

11 a–c.   *C.V.* Bibliothèque Nationale, fasc. 1, III He. Pl. 46, 5, 6, 1.
        Cf. also Haspels, *Attic Black-figured Lekythoi*, p. 10.

12 a and b. Rumpf, *Chalkidische Vasen*, Pls. xv, xiii.
Cf. also *British Museum Catalogue of Vases*, ii, p. 110; Pfuhl, figs. 161–165; H. R. W. Smith, *The Origin of Chalcidian Ware* (1932).

13 a. *Wiener Vorlegeblätter*, 1889, Pl. 4, 1b.

13 b. Phot. Mansell.
Cf. also Beazley, *Attic Black-figure: a Sketch*, pp. 21, 34; *J.H.S.* 1931, pp. 256–285.

14 a and b. Phot. B.M.
Cf. also *C.V.* British Museum, fasc. 4, iii He. Pl. 60, 4a and b.

15 a and b. Phot. Hellenic Soc. 3621 and C 7015.
Cf. also Richter, p. 126; Gardner, *Handbook of Greek Sculpture*, p. 144, fig. 21.

16 a and b. Beazley, *Der Berliner Maler*, Pl. 9, 1 (Heinrich Keller, Leipzig).

16 c. Phot. Museum Antiker Kleinkunst, Munich.
Cf. also Pfuhl, figs. 472, 473; *J.H.S.* 1911, pp. 276–295.

17 a and b. Gerhard, *Danae, ein griechisches Vasenbild*, Pl. 1.
Cf. also Phot. Hellenic Soc. 4992–3; Beazley, *Att. Vas.* p. 153; Harrison and MacColl, *Greek Vase Paintings*, Pl. 34.

18 a. *J.H.S.* 1912, Pl. vi.

18 b. *C.V.* British Museum, fasc. 5, iii Ic. Pl. 80, 1.
Cf. also Phot. Hellenic Soc. C542; *J.H.S.* 1912, pp. 354–369; Beazley, *Der Pan-Maler*, Pl. 5, 1; Pfuhl, figs. 474–477.

19. Fairbanks, *Athenian White Lekythoi*, i, Pl. iv (University of Michigan Press).
Cf. also *Metropolitan Museum Classical Collection*, p. 129, fig. 85; Beazley, *Greek Vases in Poland*, p. 79.

20. Phot. Rhode Island School of Design.
Cf. also *C.V.* Providence, Museum of the Rhode Island School of Design, fasc. 1, Pl. 17, 2; *J.H.S.* 1927, p. 232, fig. 7.

21 a. *Mélanges Gustave Glotz* ii (Merlin), p. 599 (Les Presses Universitaires de France).

21 b. Phot. Alex. Searl, Paris.

22. Jacobsthal, *Die melischen Reliefs*, p. 46, Pl. 28 (Heinrich Keller, Leipzig).
Cf. also *British Museum Catalogue of Terracottas*, p. 132.

23. *Römische Mitteilungen*, 1912, Pl. xi.
Cf. also *British Museum Catalogue of Vases*, iii, p. 300; Beazley, *Red-figured Vases in American Museums*, p. 153; Pfuhl, fig. 516.

24 a. *Monuments Grecs*, i, 1878, Pl. 2.

24 b. Phot. Alex. Searl, Paris.

25. Phot. Ashmolean Museum.
Cf. also Tillyard, *The Hope Vases*, No. 137, Pl. 22; *C.V.* Oxford, fasc. 1, iii I. Pl. 25, 4.

26 a–c.	Phot. Stanzani, Bologna.
	Cf. also Pellegrini, *Vasi dipinti delle necropoli felsinee*, p. 161, no. 325; *Bollettino d' Arte*, May 1934, p. 496.
27 a and b.	*Athenische Mitteilungen*, 1886, Pl. x, p. 365.
	Cf. also Collignon and Couve, *Cat. des vases peints du Musée National d'Athènes*, p. 642; Séchan, p. 110.
28 a.	*British Museum Catalogue of Vases*, IV, Pl. XIV, 2.
28 b.	*C.V. British Museum*, fasc. 2, IV Ea. Pl. 8, 14.
29 a and b.	*J.H.S.* 1904, Pl. 5.
29 c.	*C.V. British Museum*, fasc. 5, III Ic. Pl. 76, 1d.
	Cf. also Séchan, p. 149, fig. 47.
30 a.	*Jahrbuch des deutschen archäologischen Instituts*, 1896, Pl. 2 and p. 292.
30 b.	Neugebauer, p. 126, Pl. 68.
	Cf. also Séchan, p. 556; Pfuhl, § 637 and fig. 575 (Naples 3240).
31.	Séchan, *Études sur la tragédie grecque*, Pl. VI (Librairie Honoré Champion).
32.	Hermann, *Denkmäler der Malerei des Altertums*, Pl. 129 (F. Bruckmann, Munich).
	Cf. also Pfuhl, *Masterpieces of Greek Drawing and Painting* (tr. Beazley), p. 91, fig. 119; Curtius, *Die Wandmalerei Pompejis*, Pl. III (coloured); Overbeck, *Die antiken Schriftquellen zur Geschichte der Künste*, 1810–1825.
33.	Phot. Alinari, 6007.
	Cf. also Phot. Hellenic Soc. B 7343; Stuart Jones, *Catalogue of the Sculptures of the Museo Capitolino*; Wickhoff, *Roman Art* (tr. Mrs Strong), p. 37, fig. 12.

LIST OF SOME VASES AND TERRA-COTTAS IN THE BRITISH MUSEUM FOR COMPARISON WITH THE EXAMPLES GIVEN

BY TIIE AMASIS PAINTER. (Beazley, *Attic Black-figure: a Sketch*, p. 31.)

B191. Neck-amphora. A, riders setting out; B, hoplite setting out.
B52. Oinochoe. Return of a hunter.
B524. Oinochoe. Frontal chariot.

BY THE BERLIN PAINTER. (Beazley, *Attische Vasenmaler des rotfigurigen Stils*, p. 76.)

E266. Neck-amphora. Komasts.
E267. (School piece?) Neck-amphora. A, komast; B, youth with jar.
E268. (School piece?) Neck-amphora. A, Athena; B, Hermes.
E269. (School piece?) Neck-amphora. A, warrior; B, woman.
E310. (School piece?) Nolan amphora. A, warrior pursuing woman; B, old man.
E313. (School piece?) Nolan amphora. A, Zeus; B, Semele.
E444. (School piece?) Stamnos. A, Zeus and gods; B, Hermes, Hestia, Dionysos.
E468. Krater. A, Achilles and Memnon; B, Achilles and Hector.
E513. Oinochoe. Nike.
E514. (School piece.) Oinochoe. Apollo and Artemis.

BY THE PAN PAINTER. (Beazley, *Attische Vasenmaler des rotfigurigen Stils*, p. 99.)

E357. Pelike. Women with castanets.
E473. Krater. A, Centaurs and Kaineus; B, Centaurs.
E512. Oinochoe. Boreas and Oreithyia.
E579. Lekythos. Apollo and Artemis.

MELIAN TERRA-COTTA RELIEFS.

B362. Eos and Kephalos.
B363. Peleus and Thetis.
B364. Bellerophon and Chimera.
B365. Perseus and Medusa.
B366. Helle and the Ram.
B367. Lyre-player and man.

B368. Sphinx and youth.
B369. Sphinx.
B370. Dancer.
B373. Fight.
B374. Scylla.
B375. Death of Actaeon.

BY THE VILLA GIULIA PAINTER. (Beazley, *Attische Vasenmaler des rotfigurigen Stils*, p. 349.)

E186. Hydria. Goddess and two women.
E451. Stamnos. Women in Dionysiac festival.
E492. Krater. A, Hermes and baby Dionysos; B, athlete and two men.
E496. Krater. A, Triptolemos; B, athletes.

GLOSSARY

Acrotéria   Ornaments set up on the angles or on the apex of the triangle of the pediment.

Ámphŏra   A jar with two upright handles, used for wine, oil, etc., cf. Fig. 9.

Chĭtōn   A tunic, long or short, made of fine material, worn by either sex.

Chlámys   A short cloak.

Hárpē   The sword with which Perseus slew Medusa. Greek art shews it first straight, then sickle-shaped and finally as a mixture of both.

Hĭmátion   A long cloak, cf. Fig. 12.

Hýdria   A water-jar with two horizontal handles for lifting and a large one upright against the neck for pouring, cf. Figs. 18 and 29.

Kĭbĭsĭs   The satchel given to Perseus by the Nymphs.

Kráter   A wide-mouthed jar with two handles, most often used for mixing wine and water at a feast. There are several varieties: for the bell-krater, cf. Fig. 26; for the kalyx-krater, cf. Fig. 30.

Kýlix   A wide, shallow, two-handled cup, cf. Fig. 8.

Lébēs   A large bowl, cf. Fig. 6.

Lékȳthos   A jug with narrow neck for oil, cf. Fig. 11.

Métopes   Decorative panels set in the frieze of a temple, cf. Figs. 1 and 15.

Péplos   A tunic made of heavy material folded round the body and fastened with pins on the shoulder, cf. Fig. 12.

Píthos   A cask made of clay for storing large quantities of food, wine, etc. Diogenes's "tub" was a pithos, cf. Fig. 3.

Pýxis   A trinket-box, cf. Fig. 24.